CRANLEIGH
LIFE AND TIMES

MILLENNIUM
FESTIVAL

1. *A carrier's van in the Horsham Road in 1913*

SPONSORS

We would like to thank the following sponsors for their generous support in helping us to publish this book:

Attwell & Rogers, Opticians
Janet and Nigel Balchin
Mrs. Zena Bates
R. A. and M. W. T. Bracking
Audrey Broadhurst
Godfrey Callender
Cranleigh Afternoon WI
Cranleigh Lodge of Freemasons
Cranleigh Parish Council
Cranleigh Probus Club
Mr. and Mrs. C. Davis
Paul Eaton
   Goldsmith and Silversmith
Major D. S. Elliott, M.C.
Judie English
Filmarc Builders
Grahams Ltd
Gordons Fine Foods
David Mann & Sons Ltd
Mr. and Mrs. D. Magri
MDS Services Ltd
Tony and Trish Nathan,
   Nathan Photographic Studio

Natural Life
Rev. Nigel Nicholson
Nigel and Alice Osborn
Mr. and Mrs. Michael Payne
George and Kay Peacock
Mr. and Mrs. A. Potts
St. Nicolas School
Nevill Fraser Shearman
P. A. and A. Silver,
   The White Hart Hotel
Smiths Garden Machinery
Valerie Speers
Nigel Spong
   Cranleigh Rugby Club
Jan and Harry Stadler
Mr. and Mrs. A. G. Stafford
Charles Stoddart
   'Apples & Pears'
Technicraft
   Ockley Service Station
Gordon Thomas, M.I.O.C.,
   Building Consultant
John and Imelda Watts

Cranleigh Life and Times

Two Centuries of Everyday Life in a Village

U3A

**By Members of The Cranleigh and District Area
of The University of the Third Age**

Edited by:
Muriel Longhurst, Michael Miller, Anne Woodford and Chris Baker.

Computer services : Chris Baker

ISBN 0 9536183 0 7

Published by Cranleigh and District U3A,
Cranleigh, Surrey
1999

Produced by Wellset Repro Ltd., Grantley House, The Common, Cranleigh, Surrey GU6 8RZ

CONTENTS

───────── ○ ─────────

'He was – what I often think is a dangerous thing for a statesman to be – a student of history; and like most of those who study history, he learned from the mistakes of the past, how to make new ones'

A. J. P. Taylor

LIST OF ILLUSTRATIONS

PREFACE

This volume is the result of more than two years' work by a group of members of the Cranleigh and District branch of the University of the Third Age who met to study and to compile a picture of community life in Cranleigh to commemorate the Millennium. Original documents such as parish registers, censuses, trade directories and parish magazines have been used for research and interviews with local people have enriched our enquiries into the more recent past. The book's focus is on aspects of continuity and change in community life in the nineteenth and twentieth centuries, a time period chosen because it is well documented and therefore easier to research.

The centre of interest is not the buildings or institutions, nor is it about 'the great and the good'. It is essentially about the community. The aspects of change, and indeed, of continuity, that we have studied, are of course, only a small part of the total picture. In looking at communications, families, shopping, schooling and the hospital, we have tried to deal with a few of those aspects of life in a community that touch all our lives, and with which most people can readily identify. That they represent the choice of the group is no accident. This is a book about the people of Cranleigh, written by a local group whose members have, collectively, many years' experience of life in Cranleigh. There is much that we have discovered and much that we have left undone. Our hope is that readers will find in it something to enrich, deepen and challenge their understanding of the past history of this community as we look forward to the new millennium.

CHAPTER 1

INTRODUCTION

This book looks at life in Cranleigh over the last two centuries, a period of immense change in every aspect of people's lives. The leap forward in technology alone has altered every moment of our lives and attitudes to equality, the right to good health, education and the democratic process have shaped a community with characteristics quite alien to those of previous generations.

How was the community seen in the early nineteenth century compared to now? We have concentrated on the parish of Cranleigh, but it is impossible to ignore the national and even the international picture. No community develops in isolation.

The Cranleigh of 1800 was a small agricultural community. Fifty years later, the census of 1851 shows that the population had increased by about half, and by the end of the century it had more than doubled. Now, after nearly another century, it has a population of over 13,000 and is, in effect, a small town, with a wide range of amenities, shops, banks, library, hospital, schools, leisure centre, to name but a few. Its inhabitants follow a wide range of occupations, not only in Cranleigh itself, but travelling and working all over the UK and indeed, all over the world. At the beginning of the nineteenth century, Cranleigh was in the hundred of Blackheath and parish affairs were run by the vestry, who were responsible for many things including the administration of the Poor Laws, the Workhouse, law and order and road repairs.Towards the end of that century, the vestry was replaced by the parish council, now just over a century old, and Cranleigh is now part of Waverley Borough, itself part of Surrey County Council. Both these organisations are young within the timescale of Cranleigh's history.

These changes in the ways people's daily lives were regulated are simply examples of how Cranleigh, in common with the rest of the country, has over the last two hundred years, seen a pace of change perhaps greater than in any other period of its history.

The Napoleonic Wars of 1793 to 1815 brought rises in the price of food; enclosures between 1750 and 1850 changed the way of life in the countryside; net food imports paid for by increasing exports of manufactured goods during this period affected the relationship between the population and the land, with the result that by about 1851 half the country's population was urban. The nineteenth century in England saw the end of the reign of George IV, and the long reign, from 1837 to 1901 of Queen Victoria. Her rule brought the time of 'family values' and Victorian virtues. The Great

Exhibition of 1851 displayed products and designs from all over the world. The first half of the century had brought steam ships, the electric telegraph, and perhaps the most significant in terms of its impact on the country, the railway. The nature of communication and travel across the world had altered more rapidly than ever before.

By 1859 England was just entering on a long period of peace and Victorian material prosperity.The Great Exhibition of 1851 was now just a memory and the Crimean War and Indian Mutiny just over, although the after effects were still apparent. Movement to the cities brought its own problems of poverty and disease. Despite growing wealth and prosperity many were beginning to be concerned about the aftermath of the industrial revolution and its effects upon the lives and conditions of the less fortunate members of society. Shaftesbury was concerned at conditions in factories and more notably the employment of children. Dickens was highlighting the inequalities of society, the poverty of the working classes and the general miseries of town and country life. In agriculture too, the introduction of mechanisation had created problems with the increase of accidents to farm workers.The construction of railways also brought their toll of accidents.The efforts of philanthropists, concerned about issues such as health, poverty and education, affected national legislation, and brought about significant changes in local areas. In Cranleigh this was reflected in the building of the National School in 1847 and the Hospital in 1859.

One important area of legislation was that of education. The Education Act of 1870, for example, was a turning point for the young. It enforced the building of schools for elementary education where existing provision was inadequate, aiming to provide a school place for every child. In areas without adequate voluntary (church) schools, board schools were to be set up run by a board of governors. It was also the last opportunity for churches to claim building grants. This prompted a spate of building, not least in Cranleigh, as we shall see. However, education was still not compulsory or free and further Acts of Parliament and local bye-laws were needed to enforce attendance. It was not until 1944 that secondary education became available to all.

The Illustrated London News of Saturday April 5th 1851, discusses how the census of the preceding Monday will show 'not only how many men, women and children we are in Great Britain, but in what manner we are all enabled to live'. The article goes on to discuss the then great occupations of agriculture, and staple manufacturing industries of cotton, woollen and hardware, which 'carry our name and fame and usefulness to the remotest regions of the globe'. It talks of 'the extent of the feud between the "haves" and the "have nots",' and of the responsibility of statesmen to seek remedies for poverty if there is more of it 'than is consistent with sound economy and justice to all classes'. Similar concern is expressed about the ignorance of our children by comparison with those of other nations, and the reasons for crime and possible remedies. These issues and others brought more closely under scrutiny by the increased record keeping of Victorian times have been the subject of both legislation and philanthropic endeavour up to the present day. By the end of the century some action had been taken on many of these issues. But in spite of much progress many of the social concerns expressed in 1851 are still ours today.

In the twentieth century, within memory of many adults alive today, we have had two world wars, and recovered from them. We have seen the growth of travel, and of the motor car, and man has set foot on the moon. Technological marvels abound, developing at an ever faster pace. Most households now have televisions and cars, information technology is an integral part of all our lives, and people are accustomed to flying as a means of transport.

The enfranchisement of all men over 21 and women over 30 in 1918, has led to more changes in the democratic process. Now the voting age for all is 18, and we have had our first woman Prime Minister. 1951 saw another great exhibition, the Festival of Britain, held on the South Bank of the Thames in London. As at the end of the nineteenth century, the twentieth is ending with a queen on the throne, the reign of Elizabeth II spanning the years from 1952 to the present time.

What effect has this national picture had on Cranleigh? We are talking about a geographical area defined as the parish of Cranleigh, but a community is not necessarily a geographical concept. Community life is made up of a complex interaction of many factors. Belonging to a community involves people in all kinds of ties and common interests. Leisure, as well as work, religious as well as secular power, law and order as well as crime, local customs, and many more such concerns touch our daily lives. Most importantly, a community is made up of people. Families are at the heart of a community. Their relationships and interactions generally influence to a considerable extent how the community works as a whole. Community history investigates these interactions, whereas local history describes a locality.The work which follows is only a starting point in an attempt to understand more fully the lives of our forebears. Communications, family life, education, the hospital and shopping habits have changed out of all recognition over the last two hundred years.

Previous generations of Cranleigh residents have left us many records that enable us to learn about their lives. The vestry, the forerunner of the parish council, which managed the life of the village, left us minutes detailing its work from 1820 onwards. We have Poor Rate records, parish registers which tell us about births, deaths and marriages, trade directories show much about the local businesses of the time and we have documents relating to individual institutions such as the hospital and the school. There are deeds to many buildings, maps, including a tithe map, and many other records such those of the quarter sessions. Many more personal documents such as wills and marriage settlements, relating to individual families, also exist. Some of these are preserved in the Surrey History Centre, or in national archive collections; others are treasured by individual owners or businesses, while yet more may probably be still undiscovered. It would be the work of many years to investigate the wealth of information about Cranleigh's past which all these treasures hold.

We hope our readers may be interested enough to follow up those areas of investigation which we have left untouched, or to investigate more thoroughly those where we have made a beginning.

CHAPTER 2

COMMUNICATIONS

EARLY ORIGINS

In prehistoric times the area where Cranleigh now stands was part of the vast Wealden forest and was known to be a most inhospitable place frequented only by wild animals. When he arrived in this vicinity man chose to settle on the high ground overlooking the Tillingbourne Valley. The need to renew supplies of timber and provide grazing for animals meant that clearing of the nearby forest became essential to survival. Many of the ancient trackways in the region which follow a north - south orientation provide testament to this early need to travel. Some of these early clearings became settlements and it is from these that the name 'fold' or 'lea' derives. The road from Shere over Winterfold to Ewhurst is one such example. [1]

The main route established by the Romans between London and Chichester passed to the east of Cranleigh and sections of the original route are still visible at Ockley. Hillaire Belloc in his monograph on the Stane Street [2] describes a branch from Rowhook to the temple at Farley Green. Traces of a Roman villa, pottery, and a brick and tile making kiln have been found near Ewhurst but no substantial evidence of any Roman settlement in Cranleigh.

The Norman knights who came from France with William the Conqueror were granted large parcels of land in which to establish their manorial rights. According to the system of tithes they became entitled to collect one tenth of all crops produced by the tenant farmers and in return were bound to provide a centre for Christian worship, administered by a priest or rector, who in turn was entitled to a portion of the tithe. It seems likely that St. Nicolas church was established close to its present position to provide such a place of worship for the estate workers and tenant farmers of the area.

Cranley is not mentioned in the Domesday survey of 1086. For the next seven centuries or so it remained a small isolated agricultural community, its prosperity being hampered by the clay soil which made movement in the area during the heavy winter rains virtually impossible. Goods bought in from the neighbouring towns arrived by pack mule and even then it was often necessary to lay tracks of faggots on the soft ground.

Isolation does carry its advantages. Its remoteness probably accounts for why the scourges of the Black Death and the Plague seem to have passed by with little effect on the life of the village. The Civil War and political unrest do not appear to have left their mark although we do know that Oliver Cromwell stayed at Knowle House with a detachment of troops and granted the right to hold an annual fair as a token of his appreciation.

To understand where a community is positioned in relation to its surroundings it is first necessary to view it as part of a hierarchy of places, all to some extent dependent on each other and each fulfilling a recognised role in the functioning of the local community.This concept known as Central Place Theory [3] has been used by local historians to predict the existence of five levels of communities with differing degrees of importance or functionality determined by the extent of the services offered and not just the size of the population. We can test this working hypothesis by considering the position of Cranleigh in relation to its surrounding communities in the south-west Surrey area.

Guildford

It is clear that Guildford satisfies all the criteria for what is referred to in the theory as a High Order Centre. Its early origins lie in its position as a river crossing for the ancient trackway running east to west between Winchester and Canterbury. Later the medieval guilds were established here and it became the major administrative area for the whole region, its supremacy being challenged only by Kingston with the establishment of County Hall. Guildford itself has benefited from its position on the main route from London to Portsmouth with its harbour and naval dockyard. The town's trade was further enhanced with the opening of the Wey and Arun canal and Dapdune Wharf but the coming of the railway possibly had a lesser effect. When the Southampton railway passed through the less densely populated areas to the north it impacted more obviously on the relatively small village of Woking.

Market Towns

A second order of importance can be determined by reference to market towns which are connected to Guildford by trunk routes most of which remain in regular use today. Maps of the 18th century indicate the existence of fourteen market towns in Surrey. Those that fall within the sphere of influence of Guildford are Farnham, Chertsey, Dorking, Haslemere, Godalming and Horsham in Sussex.

Reference to the map shows quite clearly the central role played by Guildford and the towns are disposed fairly regularly within a radius of some 9 -16 miles. Thus no point is further than 5 - 8 miles away from the nearest market, this being the distance a farmer would be prepared to travel to market and back in one day, bearing in mind that it may also be necessary to drive a flock of sheep or a herd of cows. Markets placed closer than this would not survive as they would not be able to offer the range of wares or the number of potential purchasers. The obvious exception is

GUILDFORD AND ITS MARKET TOWNS

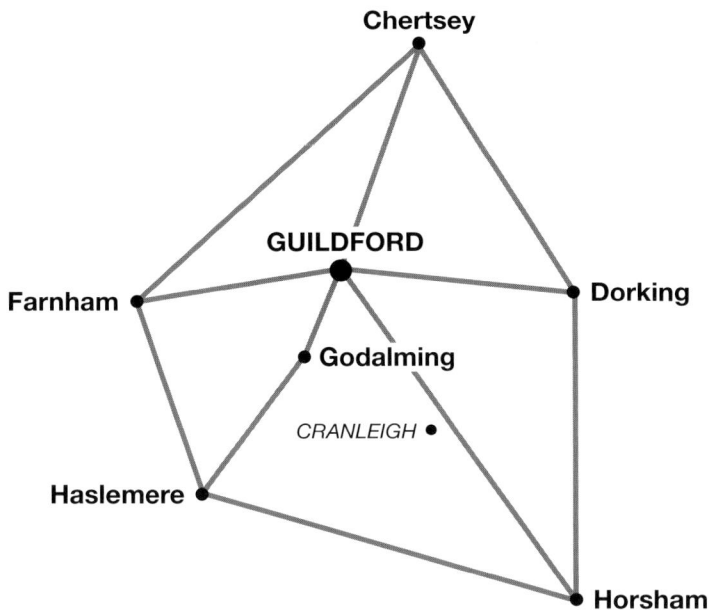

Chertsey

GUILDFORD

Farnham

Dorking

Godalming

CRANLEIGH

Haslemere

Horsham

Godalming (5 miles) which has a significant history of its own based on an important wool and textile industry originating in the Middle Ages. Clearly there is no regular hexagonal array as might have been predicted by Central Place theory but irregular topography and the influence of the main axis between London and Portsmouth have had their effect.

The Middle Order

The middle order is represented by what today we would recognise as a large village or small town such as Cranleigh. People living in a rural community become accustomed to having most of their basic needs available locally. For a wider range of goods and services travel to a higher order centre, such as Guildford or Horsham, may be necessary but the middle order in turn provides services for its own hinterland. Inhabitants of smaller local villages look to Cranleigh to provide supermarkets, banks, jewellers and leisure facilities like the cinema and sports centre.

The number and variety of traders in Cranleigh can be traced back to the middle of the nineteenth century by reference to contemporary trade directories [4] which are summarised in the table over.

In choosing 1851 we can begin to see the effects of the improving road transport system on the village and the ability of the carrying trade to support supplies to what is essentially still a rural community. By 1903 the use

7

GROWTH IN TRADE 1851 TO 1903
Number of Traders listed in Kelly's Directories

	1851	1903		1851	1903
Shopkeepers and Traders			**Manfacturers/ Wholesalers**		
Grocers	5	10	Timber Merchant	1	2
Bakers	4	5	Corn Merchant		1
Butchers	2	4	Seedsman		2
Victuallers, wine and tobacco, includes innkeepers	3	6			
Beer retailer/brewer		5	**Professional**		
			Doctor	1	3
Foodstuffs (Manufacture)			Solicitor		1
Miller	1	1	Schoolteachers	3	3
			Chemist	1	1
Other Traders			Auctioneer	1	1
Carriers	3	2			
Coal Merchant		2	**Clerical**		
Furnisher		1	Registrar	1	1
Ironmonger		1			
Remover		1	**Service Workers**		
Stationer		2	Postmaster	1	1
			Carman		2
Skilled Craftsmen			Fly Proprietor		1
Builder and Supplier	5	10			
Carpenter		1	**Arts**		
Tailor	2	2	Artist		1
Clothier		3	Bandmaster		1
Hairdresser		2	Photographer		1
Shoemaker	3	4			
Saddler	2	2	**Other Services**		
Blacksmith/Farrier	3	2	Banks		2
Engineer		1	Estate Agent		3
Watchmaker	1	1	Hospital	1	1
Wheelwright	1	2	Insurance Agent		2
			Gas Company		1
Subtotal	**35**	**70**	**Totals**	**45**	**101**

of the railway to provide a link to both Guildford and Horsham had had a marked positive influence in providing not only goods and services but an immigrant population with new skills and hitherto uncalled for requirements. During the twentieth century motor transport became the dominant means and the combination of car and train extended the range of the commuter beyond the Green Belt and into the 'leafy lanes of Surrey'. This inevitably brought with it the need for an even greater range of goods and services but people on the whole became less dependent on the carrier and the age of 'cash and carry' was born.

It is interesting to note that even in 1851 Cranleigh was providing services such as watchmaker, auctioneer and registrar for use by the surrounding locality. By 1903 the number of traditional trades had increased as would be expected particularly in providing the builders and suppliers to meet the demand for new homes and shops. More interesting is the number of new trades and professions that are included, notably a photographer (H. U. Knight) and our own local artist (John Clayton Adams). The brewing and retailing of beer is clearly well supported and the estate agent and solicitor have arrived on the scene.

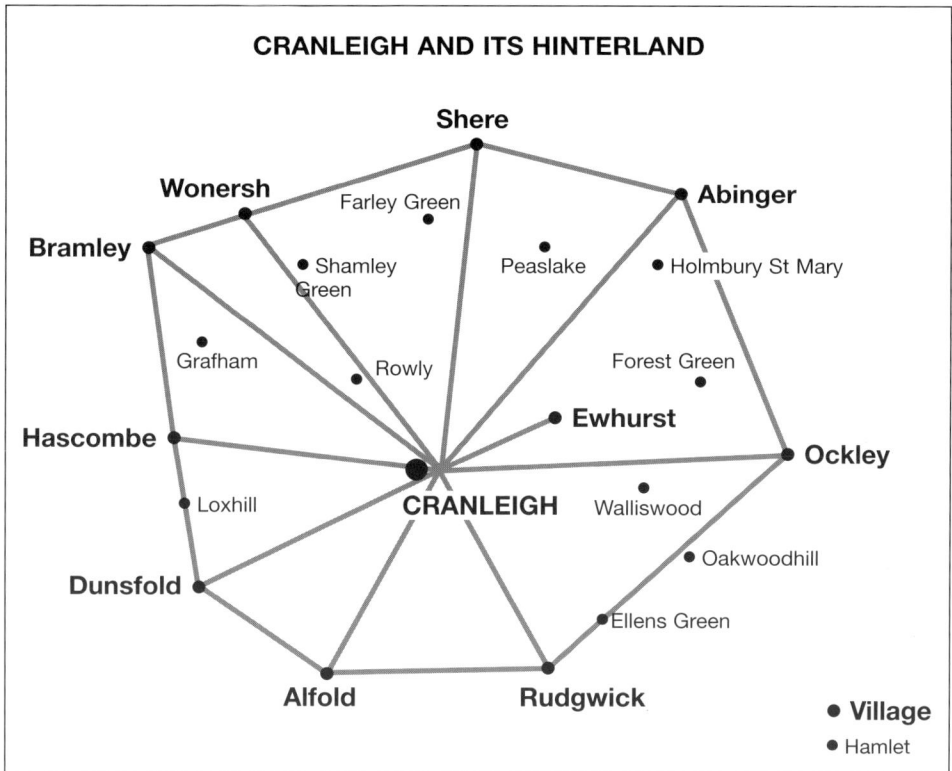

CRANLEIGH AND ITS HINTERLAND

Shere

Wonersh

Farley Green

Abinger

Bramley

Shamley Green

Peaslake

Holmbury St Mary

Grafham

Rowly

Forest Green

Hascombe

Ewhurst

Ockley

Loxhill

CRANLEIGH

Walliswood

Dunsfold

Oakwoodhill

Ellens Green

Alfold

Rudgwick

● Village

● Hamlet

Surrounding Villages

A fourth level in the hierarchy is represented by the villages which surround Cranleigh and rely upon it to provide services in addition to those available locally. In former times such a place would typically have enjoyed the services of a baker, general stores and post office, a church and at least one inn or public house. Other important centres of village life were the smithy and the wind or water mill now sadly confined to realms of history. At the time of the Domesday Survey Bramley was an important place compared with Cranleigh which did not warrant a mention. Wonersh also enjoyed considerable prosperity as a centre of the wool trade during the sixteenth century but the positions had reversed by the middle of the

TRADERS LISTED IN KELLY'S DIRECTORY		
	1851	1903
Cranleigh	44	101
Bramley	26	50
Rudgwick	20	40
Ewhurst	18	36
Wonersh	19	24
Dunsfold	17	23
Alfold	6	22
Shamley Green	2	18
Hascombe	4	10

Trades and services for Cranleigh and surrounding villages

nineteenth century as the table shows. Could it be that their proximity to Guildford meant that they were less able to support a wide range of services in their own right?

The Hamlet

A lower hierarchical level of small villages and hamlets is typified by Rowly, Ellens Green, Loxhill and Forest Green. Shamley Green was little more than a hamlet in 1855, its church having been built in 1863. [5] By 1903 it had clearly been discovered and warranted an entry in the directory in its own right. In the subsequent sections we intend to show how the development of transport and communications influenced the growth of Cranleigh in relation to surrounding localities.

ROADS

The increasing need for improved roads led to the formation of Turnpike trusts.These private companies were authorised by separate Acts of Parliament to build and maintain roads between set points and to charge a small toll for use at the turnpike gate at each end of the road. The first Turnpike Act was passed as early as 1663. Between 1700 and 1750 as many as four hundred Road Acts were passed; between 1751 and 1790 sixteen hundred. [6] Subscribers to the Trusts were in the main farmers and gentlemen who hoped to benefit from the construction of the road.

At that time a 'metalled' surface was a far cry from the roads we take for granted today. John McAdam's method of using small angular stones which were bound together rather than pushed aside by heavy weights passing over them had been introduced, but at the beginning of the nineteenth century roads were in a very sorry state. Permanent ways were established as a result of Mail coach routes but elsewhere connections between villages were little more than drovers' tracks and tended to shift as a result of traffic and poor weather making some routes impassable.

The Turnpike Road

It was in 1817 that a meeting was called in Cranleigh to consider applying to Parliament for permission to build a turnpike. The Bill's Assent was obtained on 23rd May 1818 granting permission for the construction of a turnpike road 'from the village of Bramley....passing through the parishes

Guildford 6th June 1818:

We whose Names are hereunto Subscribed do acknowledge that we have severally agreed to subscribe the sum of Money set opposite to our respective Names towards the making and maintaining a Turnpike Road from Bramley in the County of Surrey to Rudgewick in the County of Sussex and we do severally promise and agree to pay such sums of Money at such times and in such manner as we shall be required to, under the provisions of the Act of Parliament for making and maintaining the said Road —

As Witness our Hands —

Name	£	Name	£
R. B. Wolfe	300	Nichols Willm Burchatt	50
Wm Smallpeice	400	John Ellery	50
Gabriel Ryde	300	William Evershed	50
Rich Sparkes	150	William Upfold	50
Josh Baydons	200	James Child	50
John Churchman	150	Thos Hillick	50
W. Stewart	100	Richard Child	50
Lewis Potter	150	John King	100
John Elmes	100	H. P. Austin	200
Thos Puttock	200	Lord King	100
Thos Child	150	Willm Dance	100
Richd Flint	100		
John Ticknott	150		

4. _A copy of the list of subscribers to the Bramley, Wonersh, Cranley, Rudgewick Turnpike Road (1818)_   [Copyright – Surrey History Service]

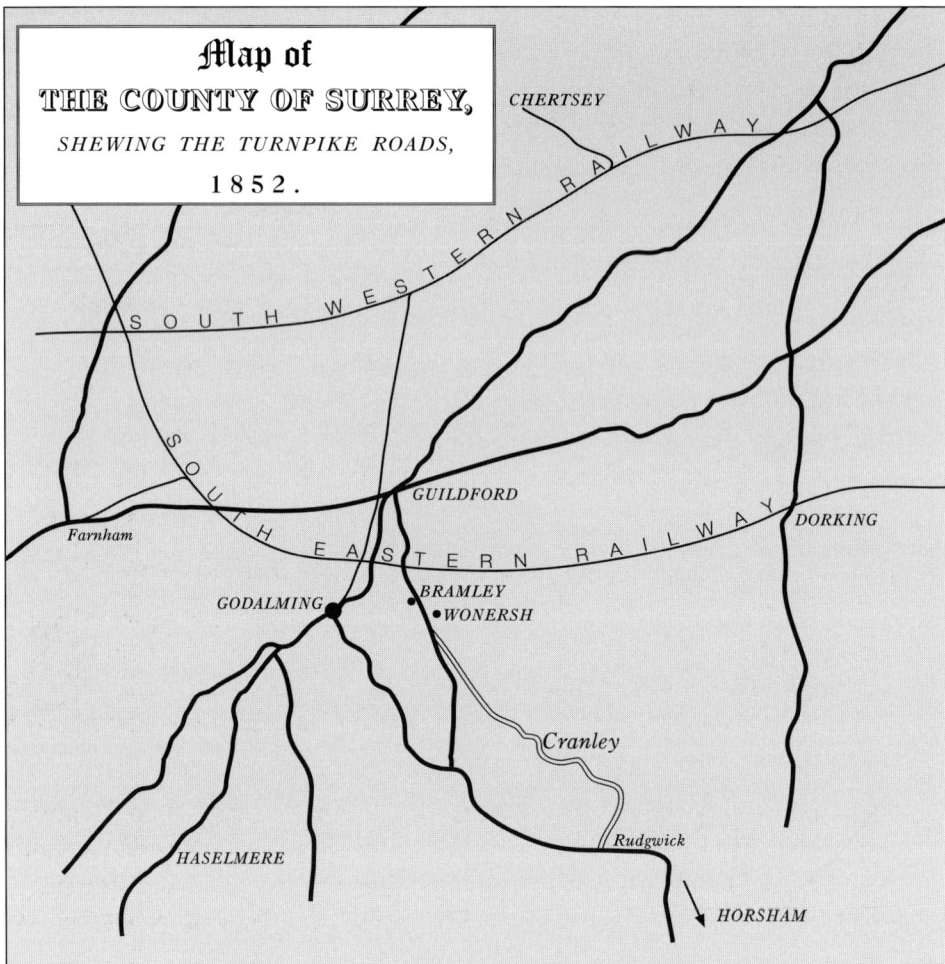

Map of
THE COUNTY OF SURREY,
SHEWING THE TURNPIKE ROADS,
1852.

CHERTSEY

SOUTH WESTERN RAILWAY

SOUTH

GUILDFORD

Farnham

EASTERN RAILWAY

DORKING

GODALMING

BRAMLEY
●WONERSH

Cranley

Rudgwick

HASELMERE

HORSHAM

5. *Map of Turnpike Roads in Surrey.* *[Reproduced by permission of the Public Record Office]*

of Wonersh, Cranley and Ewhurst to the parish of Rudgwick in Sussex, forming a communication with the road from Brighton to London, which would be a great advantage and convenience to the neighbourhood.' [7] Not only to the residents of Cranley; it is thought that the Prince Regent's desire to travel to his Pavilion at Brighton at greater speed may have been a spur to improving the road.

The building of the turnpike road undoubtedly brought income to the local farmers who provided the many loads of stone required and employment for the several toll-keepers. However income raised never reached expectations and by the 1870s most of these roads had been opened up to free use by all. A typical account of a week's traffic at Cox Green has been recorded. [8]

Some traces of the old toll-houses can still be seen at the Leathern Bottle, Ellens Green and Alfold Crossways. Pictures exist of the cottage at Gaston Gate with the turnpike across the road and the old building remains obscured by a high hedge.[9] Miss Nancy Budgett, a 93 year old resident of the village, remembers moving into The Cottage in the late twenties. At that time the remains of the old gate, a small tree and a ditch were still visible on the common outside. Early residents of the house had the advantage, like those of Knowle, of exit to the roads on either side without paying tolls.

The burden of repairs of other roads seems to have lain upon the adjacent tenants who probably had neither the means nor the knowledge to make roads. One method of mending roads was to put down faggots or bundles of heather in the ruts when they became too deep and such may have been the old practice. A serious drawback to the prosperity of farmers and of industry was the state of the roads, making access to distant markets difficult. [10]

William Cobbett, in *Rural Rides*, declared of the area in 1823, 'Now, mind, this is the real weald where the clay is bottomless; where there is no stone of any sort underneath.'

Conditions had changed very little by 1832 when a Mr. John King wrote to the Cranleigh Vestry, (at that time responsible for roads apart from the Turnpike) with reference to Hogspudding Lane, stating that the road was never repaired by anyone other than the owner of the adjoining property and that he used to 'send men occasionally to peck in the routs when the weather was suitable and they had time to do it'. [11]

In 1836 Farmer Sparkes' team which was carting manure from Elmbridge Wharf got stuck in the mud in Bedlam Lane and stopped all traffic for three weeks. As a result a road was then made to Park House on higher ground, the material for which was carted from a cutting made through Bookhurst Hill. [12]

These were the conditions in which the Cranleigh carriers maintained communications with Guildford and Horsham on a regular basis for many years.

THE CARRIERS

Standing in Cranleigh High Street as the twentieth century draws to a close, waiting for the constant stream of traffic to obey the red light and allow pedestrians to cross, it is hard to imagine a population of 1,090 in 1801 living in 'a village consisting of divers farms and cottages considerably detached from one another.'[13] Without suitable means of transport of their own the inhabitants would have relied heavily on the services of the village carriers.

> The purpose of the carrier was to unite a market town with the villages of its hinterland, with the local area dependent on it, with one another and with larger centres. He was almost invariably a villager himself operating on a quite humble scale, setting out in the morning and returning home at night, and running a comparatively light vehicle - a cart or van rather than a wagon. [14]

CRANLEIGH CARRIERS LISTED IN KELLY'S DIRECTORY: 1851 TO 1911

Date	Name	Destination	Putting Up at	Arr.	Dep.	Frequency
1851	Elliot, Edward	London	Nags Head			Th. ret Sat.
	Elliot, Eli	Guildford	Star	11	3	M,W,Sat
						Ret same eve.
	Knight, John	Guildford	Jolly Butcher	11	3	Tu,Th,Sat.
						Ret same eve.
1855	As above	As above	As above			As above
1859	Elliot, Edward	As above	As above			As above
	Elliot, Eli	As above	As above			As above
	Knight, John	Horsham	Star	9		M ret same eve
		Horsham & Rudgwick		9		Sat.
1874	Knight, John	Guildford	White Lion			As above
	Knight, John	Horsham				As above
	Streeter, Frederick	Guildford	Surrey Arms			M, W, Sat Ret same eve.
1882	As above	As above	As above			As above
1890	As above	As above	As above			As above
1903	Knight John	As above				As above
	Knight, John	Horsham	Lion, Star			Sat
	Smallpiece T.	Guildford	Lion, Star		4	M ret same eve
1911	Knight,John	Guildford	Lion			M, W, Sat, Ret. same eve.
	Knight, John	Horsham	Lion		2	M ret same eve
	Mitchell, Charles	Guildford	Star			M, W, Sat, Ret. same eve.
	Stedman,	Guildford	Star			Tu, Th, Sat, Ret. same eve.

Extracts from Kelly's Directories 1851 – 1890 showing Cranleigh Carriers Schedules

Many carriers had no other occupation, while others combined the role with another job. Farmers appear as carriers quite frequently in trade directories and others had close agricultural ties, such as Frederick Streeter, the long serving meal-man of Cranleigh. [15]

Routes, days and times remained constant even if the carriers changed. When a carrier died or retired his place was taken by another village resident who maintained the same timetable. The carriers lists, such as the Guildford Almanac [16], reveal that some carriers not only served the same villages but also arrived in and departed from Guildford at the same time, which points to the likelihood that they travelled together. The West Surrey countryside was still wild and lonely, and although by 1850 highway-men and robbers had disappeared, a long held practice would linger on. [17]

It was this continuity and reliability of the service offered to regular customers which were the building blocks of the carrying trade. Gertrude Jekyll, writing in 1904, states that 'now the carriers carry note-books, but the older men, who could neither read nor write, could remember and they would fill their vans with their many commissions without forgetting anything or making a mistake.' [18]

Throughout the period 1854 - 1902 it was normal for carriers to and from Guildford to operate from one of the inns in the town. These provided excellent facilities in respect of cart loading, stabling, refreshment and for passengers a conspicuous landmark and shelter.

Edward Elliott, born in 1811, lived at Luck's Green and in 1851 was the only Cranleigh carrier recorded as running a service to London. Between 1851 and 1859 he left every Thursday, putting up at the Nags Head, Borough, and returning on Saturday. Between 1847 and 1868 his occupation is variously recorded as both carrier and farmer and it is likely that he combined both jobs, carrying his own produce and that of his neighbours.

Edward's brother, Eli, was also a carrier plying between Cranleigh and The Star in Guildford on Monday, Wednesday and Saturday returning the same evening. His residence was given in 1848 as Cranley Village. Both brothers died in 1868.

A John Knight appears in the 1841 census aged 25 living in the household of Jacob Ellery, surgeon, in Cranley Street, as a manservant. Between 1851 and 1867 he appears in the parish registers as the father of nine children born to Emma Chapman, his first wife, Mary, having died in 1846. As will be seen from the table, a John Knight continued as a carrier between Cranleigh, Guildford and Horsham right through until 1911 and it seems likely that several generations were involved. In the first half of this century the family lived at Jenkins Farm on the Horsham Road and the stable for horse and van can still be seen.

Although they are not listed in trade directories, James Lee was another local carrier in the nineteenth century, as was Tom Beadle who also carried to London, and whose family is described in a later chapter.

Legislation in the 18th century empowered magistrates to set maximum rates of carriage, but by the 19th century the competition between carriers did the job for them. They looked to each other when they wished to raise prices. There was a distinction between 'gents' and trade price. Anything sent by or to a gentleman could be anything up to half above trade price.

6. Lithograph of Guildford High Street with the wagon of Knight, the Cranleigh carrier, in the centre of the picture (1877)

Provender for horses, with its seasonal fluctuations, was a major factor in the cost of running a carrier's business, dependent as he was on the health and well-being of his horses. [19] Toll charges, when the Turnpike roads came into being, must have been taken into account, but would have been off-set to some extent by the improvements these roads provided - better surfaces, wider roads and easier gradients, easing the horses' labour.

Two alternative forms of transport also reached Cranleigh. The Wey and Arun Junction Canal was in operation between 1816 and 1871 and a branch of the London, Brighton and South Coast Railway was opened in 1865. While they took trade from the heavy long-distance wagons, the need for the services of the local carriers is likely to have increased. Their business was greatly stimulated carrying goods and passengers from the local rail-head to the villages, hamlets, farms and industries within the hinterland of many a market town, and the carriers remained to provide vital links for the inhabitants of an area well into the 20th century, when motor transport took over. With the railway falling under the axe of Dr Beeching in 1965 Cranleigh once again became dependent on road transport.

Reference to Kelly's directory of 1938 shows a Mr. H. T. Dicker operating from premises in the Guildford Road (near to Gaston Gate) between Guildford and Cranleigh twice a week and London once a week. Local business man Gordon Thomas recalls that even in the late sixties Mr. Dicker would travel to Guildford to collect a single pane of glass for a cus-tomer and deliver it to Cranleigh the same day. A Mr. A. D. Paine operated a service from Alfold Road. In the late twenties, Mr. William (Bill) Pescud operated from his house in the Ewhurst Road, and the picture shows him with his van.

7. *The van of W.G. Pescud, a Cranleigh carrier, in the Ewhurst road in the 1920's*

CANAL

The Wey and Arun Junction Canal linked the Wey Navigation at Shalford with the Arun Canal at Newbridge near Wisborough Green and was opened for traffic on 29 September 1816. Its history is well documented in

London's Lost Route to the Sea by P. A. L. Vine. From a companion work, Surrey Waterways by the same author we learn: 'Its total length was 18½ miles and the main engineering works consisted of 18 locks, over 30 bridges and two small aqueducts at Bramley and Drungewick.' [20] Quite an undertaking at a time when most of the work was done by hand and the muscle provided by the 'navvies' who were paid a pittance for such hard graft. The cost of over £100,000 was raised by the issue of shares, the largest holder being the 3rd Earl of Egremont of Petworth House.

The Act of Parliament to aquire the necessary land was finally passed in 1813 no doubt spurred on by the perceived need to provide an alternative route to the sea in the event of Napoleon blockading the English Channel. Of particular significance to Cranleigh was the construction of the wharf at Elmbridge which allowed the import and export of a variety of materials necessary for the growth of the community such as lime, coal, grain, and timber. In June 1819, to encourage the coal trade, the Arun Navigation reduced tolls from 3s to 2s 6d per chaldron on traffic bound from Littlehampton to Elmbridge Wharf, Cranleigh.

The Wharfinger at Elmbridge in 1851 was James Stanton who lived there with his wife and five sons. The wharfingers controlled the loading, unloading and storage of goods at the principal distributing points along the navigations, and maintained ledgers showing all goods loaded and unloaded and rents for the use of lime-kilns, or for coal, grain, timber etc.

8. Extract from Elliots' Cash Book

stored on the quayside. Cranleigh was situated near the summit of the canal which was always short of water. Before the opening Thomas Lowndes the owner of Vachery House had agreed to allow the banks of the pond to be raised so that water could be drawn off by the navigation company. In an attempt to replenish water lost through the operation of locks windmills were constructed near Lock 17 in Cranleigh and Lock 16 in Birtley. These seemed to have enjoyed limited success as they were dismantled and sold in 1853. [21]

Very few records of the movements taking place at the time survive to this day. However a Cash Book for the firm of J. & J. Elliot, later J. S. Elliot & Son, more recently Harcros and now Jewsons, for the period 1854-59 [22] gives a remarkable insight as to the extent to which the canal was used for local trade and deliveries. At this time itinerant workers would spend weeks in the forest hewing the giant oaks and coppicing the hazels and chestnuts to produce the essential products of the day such as barrel hoops, faggots, fencing posts and rails, oak planks and oak bark for the leather tanneries at Gomshall and Gosden.

This invaluable record also shows that the firm of Elliots were joint owners of Barge No.30 with Mr. W. Stanton who later became canal superintendant at Bramley Wharf following the death of his father James. The master of the barge was one W. S. Mann and cargoes carried are typified by the list below:

35 tons of coal from Littlehampton to Guildford
3¹/₂ tons of various hoops from Newbridge to Shalford
22 tons of sea sand from Littlehampton to Guildford
17 tons of bark + 300 faggots from Newbridge to Gosden
33 tons of slate from L/hampton to Rotherhithe
30 posts and 40 pairs of rails from Elmbridge to Stonebridge (Shalford)

In 1855 Mr Jas. Stanton of Elmbridge Wharf was paid as follows:-

for counting and stacking of goods in Elmbridge	£1 10s
dues paid to Wey and Arun canal barge No.4 to Lhampton	6s
Hoops (Newbridge dues)	8s
for hacking 3393 spokes @ 3d	8s 6d
Total	£2 12s 6d

Other regular stopping places in the local area were Rushett Bridge, Run Common, and Compasses Bridge. As early as 1856 there were ominous signs for the canal when various parts for the railway were transported from the sea port of Littlehampton to Catteshall on the outskirts of Godalming.

	May	17	37½ tons of Iron Rails
	Jun	24	25 tons of Iron
	Nov	18	36 tons of Iron
1857	May	21	17 tons of Railway parts

These were destined for the extension of the Portsmouth Direct railway from its temporary destination just outside the town of Godalming itself. The line finally opened in 1859.

We now know that the canal was never the financial success that had been projected and the waterway constantly suffered from lack of water, inadequate maintenance and lack of traffic. The excessively high tolls thought necessary to ensure economic viability simply served to encourage coasters to take the slightly longer, but essentially free route around Kent and into the docks via the Thames estuary. It is easy to look back now with the benefit of hindsight and claim that the demise of water transport was inevitable but the attraction of being able to move hitherto unheard of loads of 20 tons and more over terrain that was impassable to wheeled traffic for a large part of the year, must have been irresistible.

This additional movement of goods by water, until 1871 when the canal closed, no doubt boosted the road carriers' trade, as the need for connections between this and the burgeoning rail network became ever more acute.

RAILWAYS

The London and Southampton Railway reached Woking in 1838 and gave rise to the development of the modern town that we recognise today. In 1845 the branch to Guildford terminated in a field owned by Lord Onslow to the north of the town and in 1849 the London & South Western's line reached the outskirts of Godalming.

In 1860 the Horsham and Guildford Direct Railway began operations with a view to making the markets of Guildford available to the market gardeners of West Sussex. When the project began to hit problems and capital became difficult to raise the London Brighton & South Coast railway bought the stock in the company for £75,000.

After several delays the line eventually opened on October 2nd 1865. The history and description of the railway is already well documented [23], [24], and no attempt at a comprehensive treatment will be made here.

The shorter journey time from London meant that goods could be delivered from the capital in a matter of hours rather than days and the ever growing volumes of post could be delivered quicker and more reliably.

9. Cranleigh Station in the 1960s

But perhaps the greatest influence of the railway was its ability to carry people with relative speed and comfort. The convenience of this service first heralded the age of the commuter in the guise of the wealthy landowner wishing to possess a country seat without being completely isolated from business in the city. Subsequently the population was increased by ordinary folk attracted by the prospect of house and garden in pleasant surroundings within reasonable travelling distance not only of London, but of other commercial centres in Guildford, Leatherhead, Epsom, Kingston and Croydon.

The line eventually fell victim to the Beeching proposals and finally closed in June 1965, almost 100 years after it opened. Little remains of the railway today although the trackway has been adopted as part of the Downslink walking path. The old station buildings were swiftly demolished to make way for the Stocklund Square shopping development and the level of the old platforms can still be seen at the rear of the shops. The crossing keeper's cottage in Knowle Lane has thankfully survived and has been converted to living accommodation.

The period of the railway's existence undoubtedly saw the most dramatic change in the village for which the railway itself was principally responsible.

MOTOR TRANSPORT

The twentieth century saw the dawn of motorised transport and the virtual extinction of the horse as the principal means of traction on farms, waterways and roads. Once the necessity for having a man walk in front of your motor car with a red flag had been removed travel could proceed at hithero unthinkable speeds.

Records of early vehicle registrations for Cranleigh have been sadly lost but an early picture shows a vehicle registered in 1904 and is probably the first to appear in the village. [25] Clearly parking is yet to become the problem it is today and the vehicle is being driven, not by a chauffeur, but the gentleman himself. The person in uniform would have been classed as the motor servant whose duties ranged from turning the crank-handle, to opening gates and carrying out emergency repairs.

One local resident to benefit from the burgeoning motor trade was Mr. Frank Osbourn. Initially building light engines for a variety of applications on local farms Osbourn set up premises in the Ewhurst Road to repair and provide cars for hire. As the business expanded Osbourns moved to larger premises in the High Street next to the Three Horseshoes and in front of the old Bruford's Brewery building

The photo shows the premises in around 1913 and the vehicle on the left is the local bus which ran between Ewhurst and Cranleigh on Tuesdays and Saturdays. Staff in the picture are (from the left), Bill Osbourn, unknown, Frank Osbourn, Len Gorringe and Charlie Bellchamber who drove the taxi in the centre of the picture. The Model T Ford is presumably a demonstration model as Osbourns retained the sole local agency for Ford. With the demolition of the steam brewery the premises were expanded further. Osbourn's Garage later became the Cranleigh Motor Company until this was demolished to make way for the Little Manor service station.

The period following the first war saw the availability of many war surplus chassis which were converted to a variety of uses as buses, lorries and vans. The carrying trade was revolutionised by this development but more and

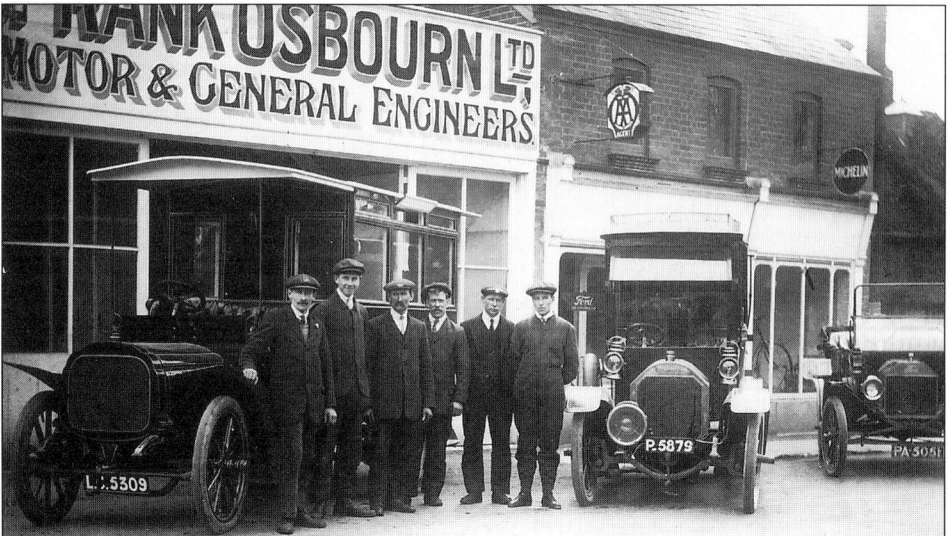

10. *Osbourn's Garage at the junction of the Ewhurst road, c.1913*

more trades were able to offer their own collection and delivery service. Goods available in London could be collected and returned the same day and removals over large distances were facilitated.

In the between wars period villagers benefited greatly from a burgeoning autobus trade provided by various operators such as Gastonia, Browns, Tillingbourne and later Aldershot & District. Services improved after the second war and travel by bus became an essential facility for commuters and shoppers alike.

The improved service between Cranleigh and Guildford was to become instrumental in justifying the closure of the railway as the latter had been in contributing to the demise of the canals. As more and more people became car owners so the road network system established over two centuries before assumed a new significance and today struggles to cope with the increased volume of traffic for which it was never designed.

It is something of a paradox that in former times the improvements in communications that led to the growth of communities is now seen as contributing to their demise, as the small local shop is replaced by the out of town shopping centre with the inevitable loss of direct links with the local community. At present this trend does not appear to have had a direct impact on Cranleigh and its surrounding hinterland which still seem able to support a strong local presence of supermarkets, small and medium sized specialised shops, a cinema, a hospital and a leisure centre.

POSTAL SERVICES

One immediate benefit of the turnpike road was that the regular and reliable delivery of mail became possible. In the first half of the nineteenth century the postal service comprised a letter carrier who collected the mail from the main office in Guildford and delivered it to premises in the village possibly stopping to pick up letters on the way. A permanent office was yet to be set up and a local tradesman would receive letters and display them in a window or make deliveries along with bread or groceries.

The first reference to Cranley in the General Post Office Minute Book [26] appears in Report No 237 for 7th November 1828.

> The establishment of the Penny Posts from Guildford to Puttenham also suggested to us the setting up of one to Cranley on the other side of Guildford and it is satisfactory to find it has produced £16.19.9 in the first year after paying its expenses - your Grace will therefore, no doubt, authorize it to be made permanent.   (signed)
>
> *J Freeling*
> (Secretary to the Postmaster General)

This appears to be the first reference to Cranley so its seems likely that the postal service was established in 1827. However things did not always run smoothly as a note for 4th August 1829 records. The Guildford Postmaster recommends the removal of the Cranley messenger on the grounds 'that the man appears to be a pauper'. Mr. Scott, the local surveyor is despatched to investigate and confirms the original report and Freeling recommends that in future 'a pauper shall not again be employed in the capacity of Letter Carrier.' and concludes: 'With your Grace's sanction this man will continue in the Service under the proviso that he is not again insolent to the Postmaster or any other person, and he fulfils the conditions of finding a proper residence.' Records show that in the middle of the 19th century the mail was transported in a small cart pulled by two mastiff dogs.

Writing in May 1838 schoolboy John Elliott observed [27] 'Some people have dogcarts and two dogs draw it and there is one dogcart comes to Cranley every morning and sometimes I have seen him get up into his cart and go almost as fast as coaches'. It appears that the mail dog cart may have attracted too much attention as a later minute records the following:-

> The surveyor was sent to investigate the enclosed complaint from Mr Stewart about the Guildford and Cranley PP messenger for carrying passengers on his Mail Cart. He had been cautioned on a previous occasion and his excuse was he had been ill and elicited the help of a friend with whom he had lived for several years in order to assist him.

Freeling recommends that he be severely reprimanded and cautioned that if the offence is repeated he will be immediately dismissed from the service.

In May 1840 Rowland Hill introduced the first adhesive penny stamp and brought the possibility of low cost postage within reach of the greater populus. In January of that year the local inspector reported:

> I beg to report a Vacancy for a messenger from Guildford to Cranley caused by the death of James Stillwell. The Wages are 30/- a week for which the person appointed will have to keep a Horse and Cart.

It appears that sometimes the temptation presented by handling relatively large sums of money proved irresistible. In 1841 William Sylvester, Post Messenger between Guildford and Cranley, was convicted for embezzling £4 14s. 6d given to him to receive a money order by Mr. Peacock. In 1842 the volume of letters was insufficient to make this a sole occupation even though a recommendation was made to increase the salary from two guineas to £4 per annum. The Minute Book does not provide a complete account of the history of the post office but the following extracts give an impression of the service at the time.

1843 29th May
D Head fined for stopping the Guildford to Cranley Mail Cart.

1848 11th April
Mr Geo Sheppard appointed to be the Messenger between Cranley and Guildford.

By the turn of the century much of the mail was delivered and collected by a postman on foot. A Mrs. Elliot, mother of Major D.S.Elliot, writing later recalls:-

When the penny post was first introduced letters were delivered around the counryside by foot.(It was before the age of bicycles.) They would be brought to Bramley very early in the morning and local postmen would deliver them to surrounding districts always reaching their destination before 9.a.m. At Palmers Cross a well built hut was erected in the rick-yard and here the postman spent the day doing boot repairs, 'snodding' as it was called, for the local inhabitants. The hut, which has now been moved to the Museum of Rural Life at Amberley, contained a chest for his tools and a coke stove by which he would sit and do his work until ready to collect the letters and do his long walk back to Bramley at the end of the day. [28]

Soon after the opening of the railway in 1865 the spelling of the village name was changed from Cranley to the now familiar Cranleigh. This was at the behest of the postal authorities in order to avoid confusion with nearby Crawley.

The local Trade Directories give the following listing for postmasters for the years for which copies are available.

Postmasters
1845	William King, receiving house. (Onslow Arms and PO)
1851	Joseph Reeves, receiver (watchmaker).
1855	Richard Crewdson (builder and auctioneer).
1859	William Reeves, receiver (watchmaker)
1867	James Summerfield
1874	John Wiggett Chapman (tea dealer) receiver.
1882	No postmaster listed.
1890	Henry Thorpe (builder)
1903	Charles Burdett postmaster

The Post Office Archives do not contain records of postmasters for sub-offices until 1920 when the Establishment records give information about length of service and salary. In considering the importance of Cranleigh in relation to surrounding villages it is worthy of note that no listing is given for Bramley, Alfold, Shere or similar places, but a James Cheeseman is listed as postman for Alfold in 1851.

CRANLEIGH SUB POSTMASTERS FROM 1920					
Year	Name	D. of B.	1st appt.	PM from	Salary
1920	L.C. Burdett	31.3.1871	1891	18.10.1897	£145
1932	W.J. Barnes	11.8.1885	1901	01.04.1931	£190
1939	A.J. Knight	1.4.1895	1913	8.11.1938	£315
1944	G.H. Wicks	4.4.1894	1911	24.11.1943	£345
1957	J.H.C. Fenton	29.8.1912	1929	26.8.1956	-
1965	H. Sparrow	18.3.1911	1929	6.7.1964	-

Many local villagers recall Harry Sparrow our friendly postmaster before he retired and moved away from the area. Post Office records after 1968 are not publicly available under the 30 year rule.

Locations

Little is known about the early location of post offices in the village since a permanent site was not available and the receiver carried on his normal trade. No information is stored in Post Office Archives and directories normally only give names of people.

William Welch in his letter to parishioners describing the village in 1846 observes that in the passage between Cranley House and what is now the Nizam Tandoori is 'Crewdson's the cabinet maker and postmaster. Alas, he is not too happy about his tenure of offices, for rumour has it that he and his family take too great an interest in the correspondence of the villagers and he is likely to lose his post.' [29]

The census returns of 1851 confirm that Mr. Joseph Reeves was both watchmaker and postmaster and whilst the location of his premises is not given we can estimate it to be in the same locality as Bank Buildings.

When David Manns established their premises in the High Street in 1887 the post office was said to be situated in the shop next door. [30]

From the information given in post office records the establishment of premises operating solely as a post office seems to have occurred around 1897 when Charles Burdett was appointed sub postmaster. Photographs from about this time show the post office to be in Ivy Hall farm. This was

11. *Cranleigh Post Office at the turn of the century, on the site of what is now 'Wine Rack'*

later taken over by Stephen Rowland and the new frontage added. The two original gables of the farmhouse can still be seen. The post office was located in the right hand section in the shop now occupied by Wine Rack.

By 1911 the office had moved to new premises in Richmond House on the corner of Knowle Lane, now Holmans jewellers shop. We know the postmaster at this time was still Charles Burdett and the telephone exchange was located above in rooms now occupied by La Scala restaurant. The office remained here until 1959 when the new premises built on the site of the old Greyhound Inn were opened.

TELEGRAPH AND TELEPHONES

The range of services offered by the post office increased to such an extent that offices were expected to deal with Money Orders, Telegrams, Savings and later still space for the Telephone Exchange. Cranleigh Post Office is registered as a Telegraph Office as early as 1874. An application affording a direct telegraphic communication between Cranleigh and Guildford was made in 1884 but seems to have been turned down by the local inspector on the grounds that:-

> the number of messages passing between the two places is about 7 in a week and since the cost of rearrangement would be as much as £50, I am unable to recommend the work being carried out. [P. O. minute book]

CRANLEIGH AREA.

CRANLEIGH.

The Exchange is open from 8.0 a.m. to 8.0 p.m. on Week Days, and from 8.0 a.m. to 10.0 a.m. on Sundays.

The Sectional Engineer, Post Office, Guildford.

1	CALL OFFICE - - -	Post Office.
8	**Briggs,** W., Draper and Outfitter.	London House.
21	**Brown,** Edward Butcher -	Common House.
24	**Browne,** Lt.-Colonel W. A. -	Barrihurst.
15	**Bruford** & Co., Limited, Brewers.	The Brewery.
12	**Chart,** H., Draper and General Outfitter.	High Street.
x20	**Elliott,** J. S., & Son, Timber Merchants.	Timber Yard, The Common.
20	Do. do. -	" Normanhurst."
23	**Goddard,** J. T., Solicitor -	Old Bank House.
2	**Grinstead,** H., Corn and Coal Merchant.	The Stores, Cranleigh Station.
26	**Hazelwood** Brick Co. -	Cranleigh.
16	**Hight,** C. W., Fishmonger and Fruiterer.	The Common.
9	**Holden,** E. A., Plumber and Decorator.	High Street.
10	**Holden,** J. H., Builder and Contractor.	High Street.
28	**Hunter,** L., Journalist -	Withybush.
27	**Kincaid,** J. - - -	Brookhurst, Ewhurst.
7	**Mann,** D., Ironmonger and House Furnisher.	High Street.
13	**Napper,** A. A., Medical Practitioner.	Broad Oak.
6	**Parsons,** A., Saddler and Athletic Outfitter.	Saddlery and Athletic Outfitting Stores.
22	**Pobgee,** R. W., Carriage Builder.	Grantley Villa.
4	**Rowland,** H., Grocer -	Post Office Stores.
3	**Rowland,** S., Estate Agent -	Estate Office.
25	**Sartorius,** Major-General, V.C., C.B.	Hurtwood Lodge.
17	**Walker,** A. H., Physician -	East Gables.
19	**Warren,** F., Builder, Contractor, and Undertaker.	High Street.
18	**Welch,** W. -. -	Stonewall.
5	**Weller** & Son, Auctioneers and Valuers.	High Street.
11	**Winser,** F., Grocer and Confectioner.	Kent House.

12. Extract from the first telephone directory for Cranleigh
(1906 Post Office Telephone directory subscribers [reprinted by kind permission of BT archives])

Telegrams were printed out in the office and delivered by a fleet of boys usually on a bicycles. Such messages were often received with some trepidation as the news was often of the death of a near relative and the service was much in use during the First World War. The facility enjoyed a more cheerful use in the sending of greetings by distant relatives to weddings, anniversaries and similar occasions but became largely redundant with the greater availabilty of the telephone and other more convenient methods.

Reference to the BT archives shows that Cranleigh's own telephone exchange was announced as opening on Tuesday 13 October 1903. This would have been situated in the shop next to Rowland's stores, now Wine Rack. In those days each public kiosk had its serving attendant whose job it was to connect the caller with the operator.

The earliest telephone directory in which Cranleigh is listed is for 1906 and this shows that the No.1 telephone was in service as the public call office of the local Post Office. [31] Personal telephones were still the province of an èlite few individuals or prominent local businesses, some of which can be seen in the following list:-

Of the twenty eight original subscribers only David Manns remains today. As more and more subscribers were added the need for more digits grew and prefixes and suffixes were attached in order to cope . The original number 7 can still be traced in Mann's present number.

In the last decade of the twentieth century the mobile phone has increased in popularity. With a new generation adapting to home based communications the need to travel may even diminish, though there seems to be no sign of this happening at present. The advantages and disadvantages of the new technologies remain to be seen.

13. *Extract 1851 Cranley census, showing the families of Knight, Ellery and Charman.*
[*Original held at the Public Record Office, Kew*]

CHAPTER 3

CRANLEIGH FAMILIES

GROWTH OF THE VILLAGE AND CHANGES IN THE COMMUNITY

Cranley in the early nineteenth century was a village in the hundred of Blackheath, with a population of about 1,000. Moule [1] describes it in 1837 as containing '166 houses and 1182 inhabitants'.

CRANLEY POPULATION FIGURES 1801 TO 1891									
1801	1811	1821	1831	1841	1851	1861	1871	1881	1891
1090	1009	1182	1320	1357	1474	1393	1830	2083	2055

Examination of the population figures suggests that there may have been two distinct periods of growth of the village during the century. From 1801 to 1831 we see an almost static population; in 1831 there is a sharp increase over the 1821 figure, the numbers remaining almost static until 1871, then a continuing increase towards the end of the century. It may be that these periods of expansion were facilitated by the improvements in communications which occurred concurrently. The canal and the turnpike road opened in 1816 and 1818 respectively and there can be little doubt of the influence of the railway's opening in 1865.

The first census was in 1801 and it has been conducted at ten yearly intervals ever since with the exception of 1941 during the second world war. The census data gives us valuable insights into the growth of the village, family structures and population size. The use of two censuses, those of 1851 and 1891, together with some evidence from parish registers, shows some aspects of everyday life in Cranleigh in the second half of the nineteenth century.

As today the responsibility for conducting the census returns was undertaken by the General Register Office (GRO) and information was gathered by enumerators whose task it was to deliver forms to all households, collecting them on the appointed day and ensuring that they had been completed correctly.

Early censuses required only the barest information. By the time of the 1851 census more detail was required and we can now discover the relationships within households, occupations of those at work, ages, though these may have been rounded up or down by as much as five years, place of birth and details of infirmity. It was the responsibility of the head of the household to supply the required information but where he was unable to complete the form it was permitted for the enumerator to assist him or even complete it on his behalf.

An enumerator was selected by the local Registrar from local residents who were literate and able bodied, not infirm 'nor of such weak health as may render him unable to undergo the requisite exertion'. The age limits were 18 to 65 years and it was specified that 'he must be temperate, orderly and respectable and be such a person as is likely to conduct himself with strict propriety and to deserve the goodwill of the inhabitants of the district'.

The four Cranleigh enumerators in 1851 were: Ebenezer Holden, born in Cranleigh, the 29 year old son of George Holden, carpenter and employer of 16 men, George Challen, innkeeper of the Onslow Arms public house, also described as tailor and farmer, born in Petworth and Robert and Thomas Butcher. They were father and son, Robert aged 53 born in Alfold, was Cranleigh's relieving officer and Thomas, his 22 year old bachelor son, was described as a schoolmaster. We can find Robert listed as relieving officer in the 1845 and 1855 Post Office Directories. By 1859 his directory entry reads 'relieving officer for Hambledon union'. It is interesting to note that three out of the four enumerators were 'in-comers' to Cranleigh.

Robert Butcher carried out the census enumeration in his own district which covered 'All that part of parish of Cranley which lies between the Turnpike Road leading from Cranley to Horsham and the lane leading from Cranley to Bucks Green including part of Cranley village' Several addresses listed are familiar today: Vachery at the start of the count to Jenkins leading towards the present High Street.

Thomas covered 'All that of the parish of Cranley which lies between the road leading from Cranley to Shere and the Turnpike Road leading from Cranley to Horsham including the remainder of Cranley Village, part of Cranley Common and Park House Green'.

A look at the 1851 census shows that there were 1474 residents of whom eight were recorded as 'sleeping in a tent'. The remainder were 774 males and 692 females, living in 281 separate households. Some idea of the isolation of village life at the time can be gained from the fact that 136 of the households were headed by men born in Cranleigh, a further 83 by men born elsewhere in Surrey, 42 by men from Sussex and only 20 (7%) from further afield. By 1891 the census shows that the population had increased to 2,055; 1,071 men and 984 women living in 422 separate households (no tents this time!). Cranleigh born men headed 121 households, those from Surrey 108, from Sussex 80 and from further afield 113 (27%). Cranleigh's isolation had ended.

OCCUPATIONS IN 1851

The work force was predominately employed in agriculture with a minority following trades and crafts such as shoemaking and other more skilled tasks. There were enough large estates in the area to support numbers of farm labourers, herdsmen, gardeners and domestic servants and most farmers could afford at least one farm servant and maid of all work. Many of the village tradesmen employed apprentices and one or even more domestic servants and the few professional families kept large households. Some indication of Cranleigh's prosperity in the mid-nineteenth century is indicated by the number of servants employed in its households. A family employing one servant probably had an income of about £150 a year. In Cranleigh, in 1851, 35 households out of a total of 282 employed at least one domestic servant.

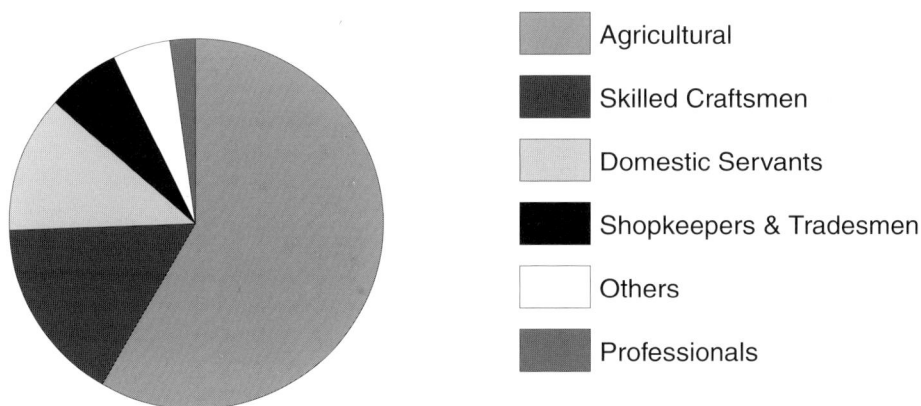

- Agricultural
- Skilled Craftsmen
- Domestic Servants
- Shopkeepers & Tradesmen
- Others
- Professionals

Dr. Ellery's household comprised two daughters and a niece and he employed a staff of four, a groom, a male servant and two females.

The Reverend Sapte lived with his wife, two sons, two nephews, and a brother and sister in law with a footman and five female servants. His wife belonged to a titled family so one may suppose that the Cranleigh rector was not dependent on his stipend alone for an income.

His curate, Edward Loring, was unmarried but employed one female servant.

John Bradshaw, J.P., lived at Knowle House with his wife and son and employed three male and five female staff as befitting a man of his station.

The remainder were one servant households. The majority of the servants were not local to the village: only three male servants out of eight and twenty one females out of forty nine were Cranleigh born. Nor were they very young, as is commonly thought. By far the greatest number were in their twenties and thirties.

NUMBER AND TYPE OF HOUSEHOLDS WITH DOMESTIC SERVANTS IN 1851	
Farmers	12
Shopkeepers/traders	9
Craftsmen	5
Professional/gentlemen	5
Labourers/Pensioners/others	4
Total	35

However, there was always the prospect of marriage. The Cranley marriage register reveals that most young women employed as domestic servants during the nineteenth century married labourers.

A survey of marriages from the register of 1837 to 1870 also illustrates the gradual improvement in literacy during the century.

1851	Grooms signed	51	Grooms marked	49
1891	Grooms signed	63	Grooms marked	37
1851	Brides signed	47	Brides marked	53
1891	Brides signed	77	Brides marked	23

The improvement in literacy of the brides is noticeable from the start of the period covered, but that of the grooms was less so and those unable to sign were almost exclusively labourers.

Farming

The majority of farms in the parish in 1851 were no longer in the hands of local born owners or tenants. A large number of outsiders had arrived to take over many of both larger and smaller properties.

William Eager from Westbourne in Sussex farmed over 300 acres at Ridinghurst; George Loveland from East Clandon farmed Bayhurst and James Tigwell came here to Utworth. We find Edward Jay from Ewhurst at Ivel farm and William Killick from Wonersh occupying Common House farm. Two of the larger farms in the area were occupied by incomers, John Whitburn with 330 acres at Maple Wood Farm and James Elms of High Upfold with 200 acres, an employer of six men. Knowle, one of the largest estates, was owned by John Bradshaw from Eccles in Lancashire who was described in 1851 as 'J.P., gentleman, magistrate, landed proprietor'.

However, there were still some Cranleigh born farmers: Henry Knight of Snox Hall, John Luff at Withybush and James Miles at Jenkins, a farm later occupied by John Knight the carrier and his family.

Although the majority of those with deep roots in the village were still employed in tasks concerned with agriculture and allied occupations the pattern gradually altered. By 1891 the predominance of agriculture had ended. Less than a third of the 422 households were headed by those employed in agriculture. At least 40% of the families were those of skilled craftsmen, shopkeepers and other traders.

When the railway came to Cranleigh there were signs of new activities starting up and once this new means of transport became accepted and its value realised there was an influx of newcomers who could see opportunities of making a good living from the local community by providing a wider range of services. These were the entrepreneurs of the day. Incomers arrived with wives and children and before long the young men and women of Cranleigh were marrying into these families thus breaking the pattern of many years standing.

NINETEENTH CENTURY VILLAGERS

William Welch's walk around the village in 1846 introduced his readers to the local community and we find young Cornelius Osbourn appearing in Cranley in 1841 as a journeyman tailor living in Cranley Street, now the High Street. In June 1844 he married Harriet, the daughter of Edward and Caroline Broomer and the register reveals that he is the son of George Osbourn, tailor, and according to Welch the young couple lived in a thatched cottage in the Ewhurst Road near the village. By 1851 we find them in Bedlam Lane. Cornelius is 35 and still a journeyman, Harriet 28 with children, Laban five years old and Thom two. We discover that Cornelius was born in Dunsfold. By 1859, according to the Post Office directory he is now an established tailor and has filled the gap left by the death of Henry Hedger, master tailor.

Over the years his family grew larger although, as was so often the case, one infant son, John, died in 1858. Happier entries in the parish register record three marriages: in 1876 son Frank to Emily Risbridger; in 1878 Lucy to William Farnfield and in 1879 Laban to Mary Botting. Five years later, in 1884 their young brother Joseph, a bricklayer, married Emily, the daughter of Moses Young, carrier of Alfold

Neither Frank, Laban nor Joseph had followed in father's footsteps to take up tailoring. Frank had moved to Gosport and was employed as a marine painter and Laban worked as a railway porter in Lambeth with only Joseph living in the village. Cornelius died at the age of 62 in 1878, Harriet having pre-deceased him by thirteen years, dying at the age of 41 in 1865.

Joseph and Emily remained in the village and lived in the Ewhurst Road in 1891. Was this the same house in which Cornelius lived forty years earlier?

They had three daughters, Emily aged six, Alice, four and Lizzie three and a lodger, William Rupert Venus, by trade a joiner.

If we move on just a few years from William Welch's walk round the village in 1846 to the 1851 census we can discover where some of the other inhabitants mentioned were born.

Amongst the tradesmen and craft workers we find Thomas Puttock the wheelwright was born in Hambledon and James Farmer, butcher, from just over the hill in Ewhurst. Henry Gumbrell, grocer and draper, was also a Ewhurst man and Henry Rowland, similarly a grocer and draper and a man of some substance, came here from Ditchling. James Warner, from Albury, has now added another line of business to his bakery, describing himself as a baker and draper and yet another grocer, Mr. Southerton, was born in Wisborough Green as were George Holden and George Laker.

George Laker was fifty four in 1851 and a master blacksmith, living with his wife Mary, born in Horsham, and children George junior aged twenty one, Harriet aged seventeen and young James aged twelve in the village main street near to Gumbrell's grocery (later Collins). George junior worked alongside his father in the forge.

George and Mary's family included four more children no longer living at home in 1851. There were two daughters and a son, Charlotte born in 1826, Caroline, who married George Pullen in 1850, born in 1831 and Robert born in 1835. The baptism of another daughter, Mary, married to James Stanford, wheelwright, in 1841 at the age of 18, does not appear in the parish register. Perhaps she was born in Wisborough Green or Horsham. George died in 1866, Mary having predeceased him in 1862. Son Robert appears to have decided against becoming a blacksmith in his youth as he was working for the local butcher, James Farmer, as a butcher's boy in 1851 and his burial is recorded in 1881.

Forward 40 years and young James is now a man of 51 and employed in agriculture, living in the Horsham Road with wife Ellen and four grown children. His 22 year old daughter Nellie is still at home and unmarried, one son James has gained employment as an ironmonger's assistant, second son William is working as a railway porter at the age of 19 and Albert, a 16 year old is a tailor's assistant. These three young men seem to have decided that work on the land is not to their liking and are hoping to make their way in more rewarding occupations.

A few villagers came from further afield. The Ruddle brothers John and James, both saddlers, were born in Wiltshire as was the village doctor and surgeon Jacob Ellery. John Snatt, harnessmaker, who lived at Turnpike gate came from Haslemere and there was even a watchmaker, Joseph Reeves, who was also sub-postmaster, from Ockley, living near the common.

Two public houses, were run by the Eede brothers from Albury, William at the Leathern Bottle and Henry at the Greyhound, and the mill on the common was in the hands of William Killick, born at Leigh.

Richard Crewdson, who was born in Haslemere, first appears in the Cranleigh parish register in 1829 when the baptism of his first child Emma is recorded. At this time he is described as a carpenter and appears as such in the baptismal entries for five more children up to 1840. In the 1841 census he is shown as living in Cranley village with his wife and five children. His occupation is builder. Next door appears another Richard Crewdson, probably his father, whose age is given as 70 and who was not born in Surrey. Richard senior appears only once in the parish register on the occasion of his burial in 1849 at the age of 82.

By 1845 Richard appears in the Post Office directory as 'Auctioneer, upholsterer, builder and glazier' so he is now a man of many talents in much improved circumstances. The building of the village school in 1846-7 was one example of his work. In the census of 1851 aged 45 years, and a master builder, he is shown as living in the village six houses away from the surgeon, Dr. Ellery, with his wife Elizabeth aged 46, also born in Haslemere and their children Charles aged 16, John aged 15, Albert aged 5 and Arthur 11 months.

Richard's eldest son and second child also named Richard, born in 1831, appears nowhere on the Cranley census so by now has flown the nest. His eldest child Emma, now 22 years old, has a separate dwelling in the village in 1851 and is described as a boarding school mistress. Her household consisted of her three sisters, Ann aged 10, Mary aged 8 and Ellen aged 6 together with a cousin and two scholars aged 9 and 5. On 13 February 1854 Emma married Edwin Foy, a chemist of Potterton in Bedfordshire, son of Robert Foy, farmer, and the couple moved away. The ceremony was witnessed by the two Richard Crewdsons, father and son, together with members of the Foy family. Richard appears twice more in trade directories: in 1851 as builder and auctioneer and again in 1855 when he has added the duties of postmaster to his other responsibilities.

Another member of the Crewdson family lived in Cranley in 1851. Headed by Charles, aged 39, born in Haslemere, with wife Elizabeth aged 42 born in Lewes and children Maria aged 11, Jane aged 9 and Kate aged 1, the family lived at Whitehall where Charles farmed 60 acres employing four men all living out. Our first sighting of Charles is in the parish register on 22 December 1839 when the baptism of his daughter Maria is recorded. At that time the family were at Baynards Lodge and Charles is a carpenter. By 1855, a mere four years after the 1851 census, Charles appears in the Post

Office directory as a farmer and has added building and brickmaking to his activities but by 1859 he is listed only as a builder indicating perhaps that he has joined forces with his brother.

CARRIERS' FAMILIES

The names Beadell, Elliott and Knight, three families who provided the carrier services in the nineteenth century can still be found in Cranleigh a century later.

We were introduced to the Elliott brothers Edward and Eli, carriers locally and to London, in the chapter on communications. Reference to the parish registers shows them as two of the children of Thomas Elliott, farmer of High Park, and his wife Mary née Muggeridge. There is no indication as to where this couple were born or where they were married but they settled in the village and raised a large family here in the first twenty years of the nineteenth century.

Edward and Eli both married in Cranley parish church, Edward to Elizabeth Wood in 1836 and Eli to Martha Edwards in 1844. Both Thomas and Mary were still alive at the time of Edward's marriage but sadly Thomas had died at the age of 73 only the year before Eli's wedding. Mary lived just a year longer and died in 1845 aged 69 years.

In the 1851 census Edward is 39 years old and farming 25 acres with the assistance of two workmen. His family comprised wife Elizabeth who was born in Edenbridge and their children: Ellen, Esther, Thomas, William and Mary, all schoolchildren. He also employed a living-in farm servant, one James Dalman, a young man from Merrow.

Living next door was brother Eli, six years younger, and an established carrier. His wife Martha was a Cranley girl and at 26 years of age already had three sons, the eldest nine year old Eli, then Arthur aged 5 and Edwin aged 2. Martha's 22 year old brother Abel Edwards, born in Ewhurst, also lived with the family.

Two of Edward's daughters married in the 1860's and Edward must have been delighted as both made good matches. Helen (seen above as Ellen) married George Sparkes, a miller of Worthing, in 1860 and her sister Esther wed Benjamin Osborn Barrington, draper of Marylebone in 1864. Esther's wedding must have been quite an occasion as four Elliotts signed the register. First came her father followed by brothers Thomas and William and lastly Mary Jane whose relationship is not clear.

Moving on to 1891, William has become a pillar of society. He is a wheelwright by trade but in addition has taken on the responsibilities of parish clerk and sexton. Now 46 years old he lives in Primrose Cottage which

14. *Primrose Cottage, opposite the Village Hall in the High Street, 1966*

readers may recognise as one of the pair almost opposite the village hall. He had married Frances Slater the daughter of Edward Slater, a blacksmith, in 1870. Both Frances and her mother were from Kirdford. By 1891 William and Frances had five children Helen, Frances, Mabel, Albert and Jack all of whom attended the village school and whose names can be seen in the school registers.

The last mention of William's family at the turn of the century is in Kelly's directory for 1903 where we discover that Helen, by now a 28 year old and as yet unmarried, is in business on her own account as a milliner.

Tom Beadell worked alongside Edward Elliott around the middle of the last century and we find him described as a carrier in the parish register at the baptism of his daughter Caroline in 1838. He was the son of John Beadell, a former London carrier, who came from Odiham in Hampshire. Tom was a man of various enterprises, described in 1851 as labourer and dealer, living in Rose Cottage with his wife Elizabeth and their children Caroline aged 13, Mary Ellen aged 9, Ellen aged 6 and three year old Thomas. Another child, Elizabeth, born in 1839 had died earlier in 1849. The household included Tom's brother George and his widowed 77 year old father John. They also had a lodger, Elizabeth Balchin, Cranley born and earning her living as a needlewoman. In this same year, Ellen was enrolled in the new village school, which the Beadell children all attended. Another son, Henry, was born to Thomas soon after the 1851 census.

15. *One of the oldest Cranleigh families is the Ste(a)dman family, first recorded in 1566. By the time of the 1851 census, no fewer than nine separate family units are recorded with that name. Henry Ste(a)dman was born in 1810 and lived in Alfold Road with his wife Ann and five children. This picture shows one of his sons, David, (b.1837) with his wife Emily (née Bravery) when they lived at Parkgate Cottages*

16. *This family portait shows William Stedman (b.1865), son of David, and his wife Alice (née Lassam). They were married on Christmas Day 1886 in St. Nicolas church and are seen here with their seven children, (back) Gertude, William, Florence, Ethel, Alice, (front) Cecil and Wilhelmena. They lived at Broadhurst cottages, Smithwood Common, and Cecil's son, Ian, still lives in the village and works as a postman*

Five years on and his father John was buried in the churchyard at the age of 82 years. Later, in the trade directories of 1855 and 1859 Tom was described as 'marine store dealer'. Tom's wife Elizabeth died in 1879 and he lived another eight years to 1879.

Forty years passed and in 1891 young Thomas, three years old in 1851, was now 43 and living in the village a few doors from Kent House in the High Street with his wife, son, four daughters and an infant nephew Arthur, aged one. Part of the premises owned by the Beadells were taken over by Manns in 1887. Brother Henry followed family traditions and was working as a carman in 1881, living on the common with his wife Emily, the daughter of Jacob Longhurst, a brickmaker. At the time of their marriage in 1875 Henry's occupation was that of coal merchant and his father Thomas whose name appears in the register was now a furniture dealer. The young couple had received the benefit of education and were able to sign their names on the occasion. Sixteen years later in 1891 Emily was a widow with five children to care for. The family lived at Jubilee Cottage. Harry was aged 13, Emily aged 12, Elizabeth aged 6, Millicent, 4, and baby Walter was less than a month old. A cousin, Emma Botting, lived with them and they were in a position to employ a domestic help, one Sarah Ann Holt, a 47 year old widow. Emily's occupation is given as carman so she may have taken on the responsibilities of her late husband in order to provide for her family.

There are still descendants of the Beadell family in the village today, and doubtless they can fill in the many gaps in this story.

FAMILIAR NAMES

It is often said locally that there are still many families in Cranleigh that have been here for generations. Investigation shows some truth in this. Taking the 1841 census as a starting point, we looked at all the names of people born in Cranleigh, and compared the list with the 1891 census, 50 years later, to see which families had lived here for 50 years. This list was then checked against the most recent telephone directory to see which families of these names appeared as resident in Cranleigh after nearly 160 years. The resulting list of twenty three names was then checked with the parish registers, to see when each name first appeared. The results are as follows:

16th century

Carpenter, William	1534	(will proved)
Stedman, John and Richard	1566	Sons of Robert, baptised

17th century

Tickner, William	1608	Son of William, baptised
Tanner, Robert	1609	Son of Robert, baptised
Edward(e), Ann	1610	Daughter of Robert, baptised
Farl(e)y, Thomas	1611	Son of George, baptised
Mann(e), Elisabeth	1610	Married Charles Lamote
Parson, Thomas (17 June)	1613	Married Ann Tickner
Lee, Susanna (9 Sept)	1613	Married William Sherlocke
Kelsey, Thomas	1617	Son of John, baptised
Knight, Ann	1620	Wife of John, buried
Luff, Margaret	1622	Married John Tanworthe
Street(e) John	1626	Married Margaret Nie
Elliott, Frances	1628	Buried
Puttock, Richard	1638	(Richard of Plistowe)
Stemp, Jean	1653	Daughter of John, baptised

It may be, of course, that some of these sixteenth and seventeenth century families were here even earlier. For example, a will, made by William Carpenter of Cranleigh, was proved in 1534, in the reign of Henry VIII. A further check of older documents may show these names appearing. We have simply used the available parish registers, which date from 1608, with some earlier 16th century baptisms. Nor have we checked lines of descent backwards from 1841 for all these families, so it may not be the case that today's families are direct descendants of families of the same name living here in earlier centuries.

From the eighteenth century, the names of Champion, Charman, Cheesman, and Hayes are listed, and from before the 1841 census, Beadell, Holden and Perry appear in the nineteenth century and are still represented in Cranleigh today. It is perhaps worth noting that research elsewhere has shown that between 70% and 85% of surnames in villages tended to disappear between the mid sixteenth and early nineteenth century. Cranleigh had 236 names shown in the 1841 census.

It is easy to see the effect of the work of the 'great and the good' and the entrepreneurs in any community, and Cranleigh is no exception. But in any community there are many who give much to the day to day life of their town or village. In Cranleigh's case, perhaps these longstanding families might serve as an example of how many ordinary people make a real contribution to community life. During the nineteenth century, for example, we can see from the vestry minutes alone, the part these families played in running the everyday life of the village. At various times, we find Puttock, Holden, Knight as constables, Elliots as clerks, the offices of waywarden and overseers of the poor, and other vestry duties carried out by Edwards,

Tickner, Street, Killick, Luff and Charman. Space is too short here to give a detailed account of all these families have contributed in the past, but there is little doubt that, for example, administering the Poor Laws alone, was a considerable administrative task, to say nothing of their other duties. Their work would repay further study. It was only when Cranleigh expanded that newer names appeared and by the end of the century, the parish council had arrived

The Poor Rate

The local community had a responsibility for the needy in the village and to this end a parish would levy rates to finance the relief of the poor. Properties were assessed for a rate, usually levied annually, and the income was recorded in poor rate books. These list all householders of every kind who were not paupers, a description of the property owned and/or occupied and the amount paid in tax.

An excerpt from the Poor Rate Book of Cranley in 1840 lists a number of familiar names.

EXCERPT FROM THE POOR RATE BOOK OF CRANLEY IN 1840						
Occupier	Owner	Description of Property	Estimated Rental	Rateable Value	Rate at 10d in £	Total to be Collected
Tickner, James	Tickner, James	Cottage, Cranley St.	£2 7s 6d	£2	1s 8d	1s 8d
Holden	Field, Richard	Blacksmith Shop, Smithbrook	£1 5s 0d	£1	10d	10d
Elliot, John	Heathfield	Cottage, Horseblock Hollow	£2	£1 15s 0d	1s 5d	1s 5d
Puttock John	Austin Sir Hy.	Cottage, Starvall	£2	£1 15s 0d	1s 5d	1s 5d

Elections

The right to vote in elections was, in the nineteenth century, still restricted to those who held a property qualification which enfranchised them. For a small village, a surprising number of local inhabitants were eligible to vote in the mid 1800s and a few familiar names from the electoral registers are shown.

ELECTORAL REGISTER FOR CRANLEY 1856/7

Name	Abode	Nature of Qualification	Description of Qualifying Property
Edwards, Danl.	Cranley	Occupier	Parkhouse Greenhouse
Edwards, Alfred	Cranley Common	Occupier	Common
Ellery, Jacob	Cranley Street	Freehold House & land	
Elliott, Edw.	Village	Land as Occupier	Stedmans Farm, Warners Farm, Selham Farm, High Upfold
Elliot, Thos,	Wisboro Green	Copyhold Land	Stedmans
Elliot, Thos.	Rudgwick	Freehold House & Land	Coldharbour
Holden, George	Cranley	Freehold House	Cranley Street
Holden, Ebenezer	Cranley	Copyhold House	nr. High Park
Killick, Wm.	Cranley	Freehold Land	Common House
Puttock, Thos.	Cranley	Leasehold House & Garden	Bedham Lane
Puttock, John	Cranley	Occupier	Hammer Farm
Street, Thos.	Mannings Hill	Occupier House & Land	Mannings Hill
Street, Henry	Cranley Common	Freehold House & Land	Underslows
Tickner, John	Cranley Common	Freehold House & Land	Barhatch

40 years on in the 1890s, many voters were still local men, but there were now more absentee landlords than in the earlier period. These were the owners of larger farms and estates, whose properties were either tenanted or managed by agents. At least fifteen farms were owned by outsiders from London, Essex, Hampshire, Brighton and further afield, as well as from Bramley, Rudgwick and other villages near to Cranleigh.

EXTRACTS FROM THE ELECTORAL REGISTER FOR CRANLEIGH FOR 1892

Name	Abode	Nature of Qualification	Qualifying Property
Holden, James H.	Cranleigh	2 Freehold Houses	Knowle Lane
Holden, Ebenezer	Cranleigh	Copyhold House	nr. High Park
Puttock, Thomas	Cranleigh	Freehold House & Garden	Cranleigh Common
Street, Thomas	Mannings Hill	Freehold House & Land	Mannings Hill
Street, Henry	Cranleigh	Freehold House & Land	Cranleigh Common
Walder, James	Cranleigh	Freehold House & Land	Rose Cottage

REMINISCENCES OF VILLAGE LIFE IN CRANLEIGH

Susan Parsons described how her family once lived in what is now the Little Park Hatch public house but when she was a small child they moved across the road to a four bedroom tied cottage, No.1 Parkhouse Green Cottages (now Stone Cottage), their address in 1891. This was one of a pair built by the

Tickners of Barhatch Lane around 1820 and James Parsons worked on the Tickner's farm.

In their new home her parents raised twelve children in what must have been very cramped conditions. In 1891 the family consisted of father James, born in Dunsfold and aged 42, mother Mary aged 40 and their children, William the eldest aged 14, Eliza, Thomas, Susan (then 10 years old), Frank, Lily, Norman, Ida and Amelia the baby of seven months. Three more were to be added to their number in the next few years.

The parents slept in one room with the latest addition to the family and the next youngest; the big girls and big boys slept in separate rooms and all the small children slept together in the remaining bedroom. There was no such thing as the luxury of a bed apiece but all the children slept 'top to tail' until they left home. The children attended the village school where their names can be seen in the registers. Later, in the early 1900's Susan's young sister Hilda, born in 1888, married one of the Worsfold family and there is a photograph of the wedding party in Warrington and Seymour's book 'Bygone Cranleigh'. Susan married into the Buckman family but there were no known children of this union.

A search through the parish registers reveals very few Parsons entries; two marriages and a baptism in the seventeenth century then nothing until a mere six entries in the second half of the nineteeth century. There are some Parsons in later census returns including John, an agricultural worker, and George, a journeyman carpenter, who both moved into the village from Wisborough Green and appear in the 1851 census. Some of their descendants appear in 1881 and 1891 but it has not been possible to make any connection between these families and Susan Parsons.

Susan remembered how on washing day the eldest girl was kept away from school to help with the laundry which was done in a copper, built into the kitchen wall. Once the clothes were washed they were taken outside in galvanised laundry pails and the clothes were mangled there summer and winter. All water used for washing or indeed for any purpose was drawn from a well in the back yard [still to be seen there today] and a privy was situated in the garden at a short distance from the back door.

Cooking was done on an open range in the front parlour and this was the only room to be heated in the cottage. Stone hot water bottles were high priority items on winter nights although sleeping three or four to a bed helped the occupants to keep warm. Lighting was by oil lamps and candles; a lamp in the parlour of an evening and a candle to light the way to bed. No reading in bed in those days!

Father worked on a local farm and was fortunate enough be able to bring home a daily allocation of milk, sufficient to give each of his children a cupful with some left over for cheese making. The garden provided vegetables, mainly roc crops which could be stored for the winter but also cabbage, cauliflowers and other greens. A few hens lived at the bottom of the garden and there were 'perks' to be had from the surrounding fields - mushrooms, nuts, hips, haws, sloes, the odd rabbit and occasionally a pheasant or hare.

Susan Parsons recollected that the older daughters of the house were expected to help with domestic tasks from a very early age and were often charged with taking care of younger siblings when of very tender years themselves. They would fetch water from the well or tap, help mother with the weekly wash when older, staying away from school on a Monday for the purpose, tend the cottage garden and run errands. Children as young as five, of very poor families, would often be required to work in the fields, picking potatoes, weeding, removing stones from the fields and gleaning after the harvest to earn a few pennies a week as a supplement to the pittance brought in by an unskilled labouring father. It was not uncommon to find the classroom almost empty during the various harvest and sowing seasons when every pair of hands was needed in the fields.

The cottage had changed little by the 1960s. It still retained flagstone floors; there was still no electricity so oil lamps and candles remained in use; washing was still done in the copper and mangled outside and some cooking was done on the range. There were a few concessions to modernity: a cold tap in the kitchen and gas had been piped in so that it was now possible to cook by gas, although the kettle was always to be found simmering on the hob by the side of the range. The garden was still stocked with vegetables and the old lady's two bachelor nephews spent their weekends digging, planting and hoeing. The two men, then in their fifties, lived along the Ewhurst Road with their widowed mother and both were diligent in helping their aunt with the tasks she could no longer manage.

Visitors would find the interior decor and furnishings were just as they had been at the turn of the century with dark brown paintwork, yellowing distemper on the walls and Victorian cottage furniture in all the rooms. There were rag rugs on the flagstones and Staffordshire fairings on the mantel, a couple of old rocking chairs and a chaise longue covered with what appeared to be rexene in the parlour, a sturdy grandfather clock against a wall and several sepia photographs on a sideboard.

17. *Impression of kitchen of 1 Parkhouse Green Cottage, c.1963* – A. Wren

CHAPTER 4

CRANLEIGH'S CHILDREN AT SCHOOL

THE NATIONAL PICTURE IN THE 19TH CENTURY

'There is no cloud so dark and so dangerous in our political system, no blot so foul upon our social system, no stain so deep upon the Christianity which we all profess, as the existence of perhaps 500,000 children who are growing to man's estate to be a curse instead of a blessing to the community in which we live.' (George Melly, M.P., 1869.)

In the 19th century there were several different types of school in Britain. For the rich and the middle classes there were private schools, which charged fees. (Cranleigh School was founded in 1865. Fees £10 a term.) But for poor children there were few schools, and many went out to work and grew up unable even to read and write. Very few children ever stayed at school after they were 12 years old.

Some went to schools built by the Churches, called National Schools (the Anglican National Society was set up in 1811) and British Schools (the British and Foreign School Society was established in 1814, linked in practice, but not in theory, to Nonconformism). The National Schools were more numerous, and in the late 1860s about three-quarters of the total grant to elementary education in England and Wales went to Anglican schools. These grants had begun at the time of the 1833 Factory Act, which aimed for children working in factories to have two hours schooling a day. If possible they were topped up by parental fees and donations from well-wishers.

In 1846, when a new Factory Act sent more children to school, a pupil-teacher system was set up. Older children taught the younger ones. In 1847 the National School in Cranley was founded. In 1862 the amount of money a school received depended on how many children in each class reached 'the standard' in the three Rs, plus a satisfactory level of attendance. Government inspectors were to carry out tests. Religious instruction also had to be given, and the girls were required to learn needlework. From 1867 additional 'specific' subject grants were offered for English grammar, geography and history, and a little later for modern languages, Latin, mathematics, science and domestic economy - but these meant little to most pupils.

Generally teachers and pupils concentrated on the minimum requirement - hence unremitting grind in the three Rs, the crushing of individual initiative, and frequent canings, even for crimes such as 'blots and finger marks'. Often schools had only one large classroom where pupils of all ages worked together. There might be as many as a hundred pupils in that one room and only one teacher. But the children who attended the Church Schools were often better taught than those who went to Dame Schools. These were run by old ladies who taught in their own homes, often with no proper seats, desks or books. Some of the women who ran Dame Schools could not even read.

The Education Act of 1870 enforced the building of schools for elementary education where existing provision was inadequate. Board Schools were set up, run by a board of governors elected by ratepayers and paid for by local rates and government money. In 1880 school was made compulsory for every child from 5 to 12 years of age. At first parents had to pay a small amount. Some even tried to trick the authorities by saying that their children had died, when really they were out at work. But from 1891 all children had free school places.

CRANLEY'S SCHOOLS IN 1846

In 1906, to celebrate the sixtieth and final year of the Rectorship of the Revd John Sapte in Cranleigh, William Welch wrote a short sketch called 'Cranley in 1846'. He set the scene thus:

> At the 1831 census the population was 1,320, and at the census of 1841 it was only 1,349 - the vast majority of whom belonged to what is known as the labouring class. Out of 28 baptisms in 1846, no less than 22 are described as children of labourers, two of bricklayers, and two of carpenters.

Welch goes on to say:

> Though schools were so many, education generally was at a low ebb, and probably not more than a quarter of the labouring class could read or write. The opportunity of education and amusement were of the scantiest, and what wonder is it that immorality, drunkenness, and superstition were rife? [1]

In his 'journey round the parish', Welch refers to five of Cranley's schools in 1846. Mr. Scott's school and Mr. Wood's school were both in the area of the cricket ground. Cranley House, where Miss Warner kept school, was where the Library now is. Her school room was a wooden out-building which was destined to end its days in poverty as the infectious ward for Hambledon workhouse. The school kept by Mrs. Fogden was near The Onslow Arms and another school was kept by Mr. Thomas Child near Dyers the Butcher. At this time few of the population were literate and anyone, however ill-accomplished, could form a private school and charge a fee.

Another source [2] refers to a dame school at Kent House, run by an elderly lady and her niece. On the door was a brass plate with the words 'Young Ladies' Seminary'. One of the schoolroom windows faced the Greyhound meadow where two fêtes were held in July. On these days during school hours a white linen blind was carefully drawn over the window facing the meadow, so that the pupils' attention should not be distracted.

In a speech in 1897 Mr. Sapte recalled the year he came to the village: 'People did not think much about schooling in those days. There were about three parts of the people in Cranley at that time who could neither read nor write. There was only a little school on the Common, which was kept by a man, who charged 6d. or 8d. per week for each boy, so that it was out of the reach of the labouring class; there was also a dame's school, and a little schooling was given at the Sunday School, but not in a very intellectual manner. The people in those days were poorly housed, poorly fed, and also, generally speaking, poorly paid.'

One of the pupils at Mr. Child's school was John Elliott, great-grandfather of today's Major David Elliott, a local farmer. Some of John Elliott's work at the school has survived, written between March and August 1838, when he was 14. As homework Mr. Child set him to write letters. In the first, John writes: 'Dear and Honoured Father, Last Saturday Mr. Child and Mr. Bennett took us squirrel hunting out by the reservoir'. In the eleventh, he begins: 'The subject Mr. Child has just given us is about a Fair.' Other subjects set include windmills, procrastination, inebriation, a farmyard, the four seasons, agriculture, vegetation, vehicles, houses, vaccination and inoculation, the sea, and shutting your ears against scandal. [3]

THE BUILDING OF CRANLEY'S NATIONAL SCHOOL

When the Reverend Sapte came to Cranley late in 1846, aged 25, there were already plans to build an Elementary Church School. In February of 1846 the Rector, presumably the Reverend Lowry Guthrie, Sapte's predecessor, had exchanged a plot of glebeland, lying off the Horsham Road, for a property described as the Old Almshouses belonging to Jacob Ellery, which, so far as can be traced, is the area that became the site of the new school. But where was the money? Since 1811 the National Society had been setting up Church of England schools all over the country for the children of poor working families, so the Rector wrote a letter to the National Society for aid towards carrying out this desirable object. Next he circulated the following letter to selected local people:

49

Cranley Rectory,
Near Guildford
March 23rd, 1847

Sir,

Understanding that you are a landed proprietor in this parish I venture to draw your attention to the fact that we are without a school for the poor. The parish is very extensive, and but very few among the lower class can either read or write.

For some time the building of a National School in the village has been talked about; and the subscriptions have already been promised to the amount of £490.

We propose to build a school and dwelling-house for the Master and Mistress by the end of the summer; but to carry out the original plans, the required sum is £610; the work therefore stands much in need of any assistance with which you will kindly further it.

I enclose a list of the principal subscriptions. The farmers have promised to bring stone from the hills, for the building, free of expense.

I trust that you will take the object into your favourable consideration, because I feel sure that it is a work tending to promote both the honour of God and the happiness of man.

I am, sir, Your obedient servant,

J.H. SAPTE, Rector of Cranley [4]

The building plans for the two classrooms, and for the house of the first Head Teacher, show that the School Room measured 56ft x 16ft and was divided into two classrooms. On one side of the Room was the Boys' Yard (60ft x 60ft) and on the other side a similar Girls' Yard, each with a swing in its centre. [5] The Head teacher's quarters were apparently most incommodious.

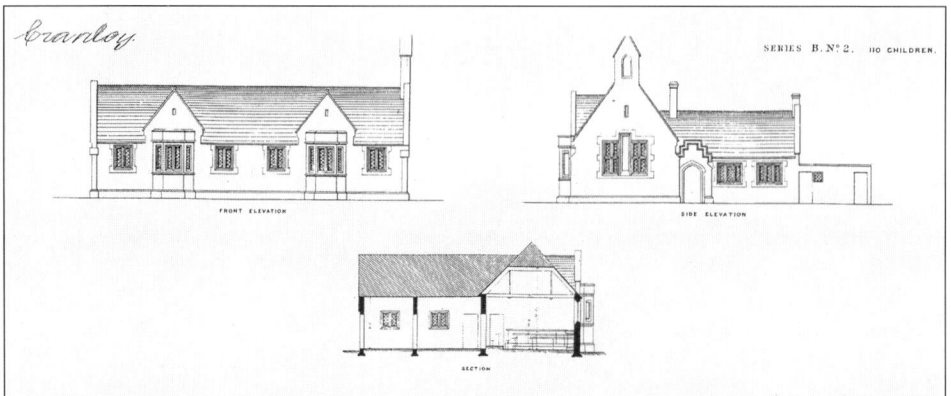

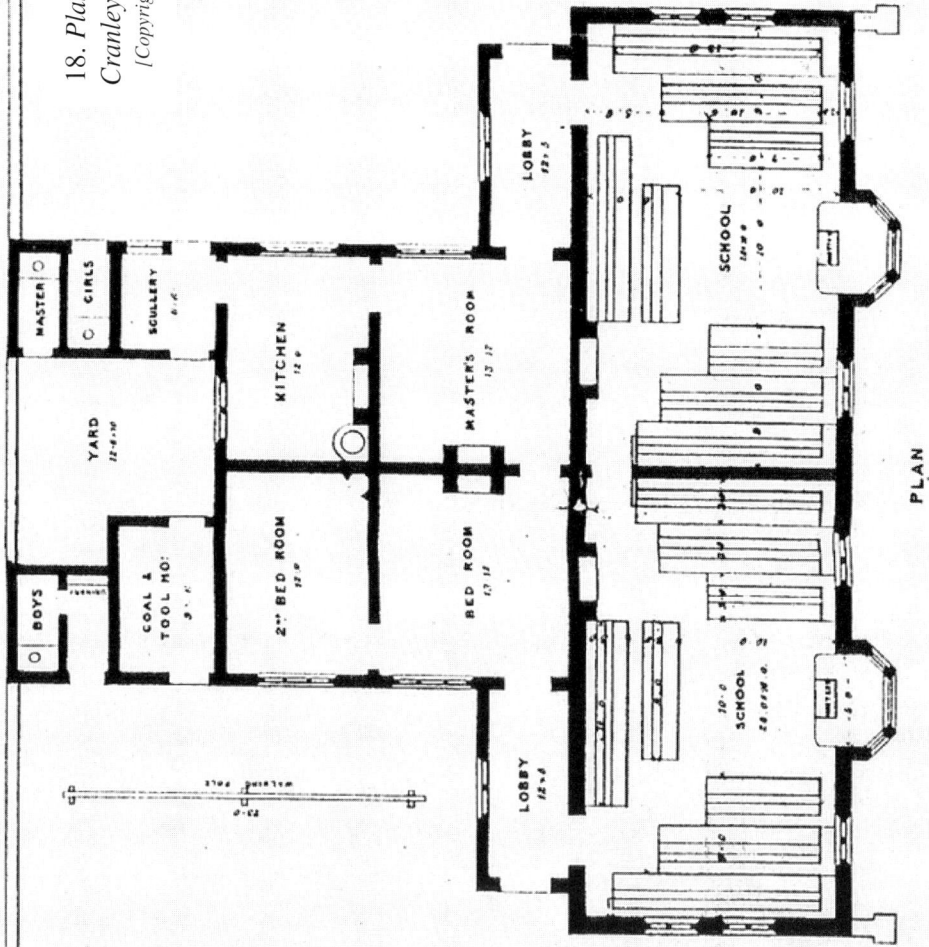

18. Plan of Original Building,
Cranley National School, 1847
[Copyright of Surrey History Service]

51

The school was built under a Trust deed. Its stone was given by the Bray family of Shere, who were Lords of the Manor, and was carted from their Pitch Hill quarries, free of charge, by local farmers. The subscribers are listed at the back of the School Account Book from 1849-75, headed by:

John Bradshaw, Esq.	122	7	0	(he lived at Knowle)
Rev. J. H. Sapte (Rector)	116	5	0	
Privy Council	112	0	0	
National Society	75	0	0	
Jacob Ellery	10	0	0	
Rev. E. H. Loring	10	0	0	[6]

Note that through the Privy Council the Committee of Council paid £112. The Committee of Council would normally pay half the cost of building a school house, but they did not have to subscribe so heavily to Cranleigh because of the large amounts raised by subscriptions. The National Society contributed only £75, and the rest of the money came in with over thirty small subscriptions. The Rector's letter had, therefore, a fairly wide response, and he himself must have been deeply concerned and aware of the need for a school to have given so generously. In the end Richard Crewdson, the contractor, was paid £639.5s.11d.

EDWARD POORE (1847-65)

Edward Poore was the first Head Teacher. The school accounts show that the Master's salary from February 1848 to February 1849 was £65, and the Mistress's was £12.10s.0d. Mrs Poore evidently taught the girls plain sewing. By 1862 the Master's salary was £80, and by 1875 it had risen to £116.16s.4d. The 1849 accounts refer to a New Vesta Stove; the school had to pay for this and for some bookcases to be made by the carpenter. To cater for growing numbers, the 1853 accounts refer to alterations and repairs. [7] For these to happen the Poores' two bedrooms were combined into the 'new schoolroom' for Infants (22ft x 12ft), into which a new Doxet stove was placed, and the Master's room became another classroom (12ft x 12ft). The kitchen (9ft x 12ft) was retained. A plan of this arrangement, drawn by a 12-year-old pupil named Edwin Peters, is shown opposite. [8]

The Early Pupils

The first entry in the Admission Register from 1848 names Thomas Mercer, aged 9, and is dated February 28th. He entered Class 1, and his 'Disposition and Attitude' is defined as 'Careless'. This register states that 119 boys and girls were admitted by the end of 1848. Entry No 72 names Frank Faulkner, a pupil-teacher at the School from May 1848 to March 1850. [9]

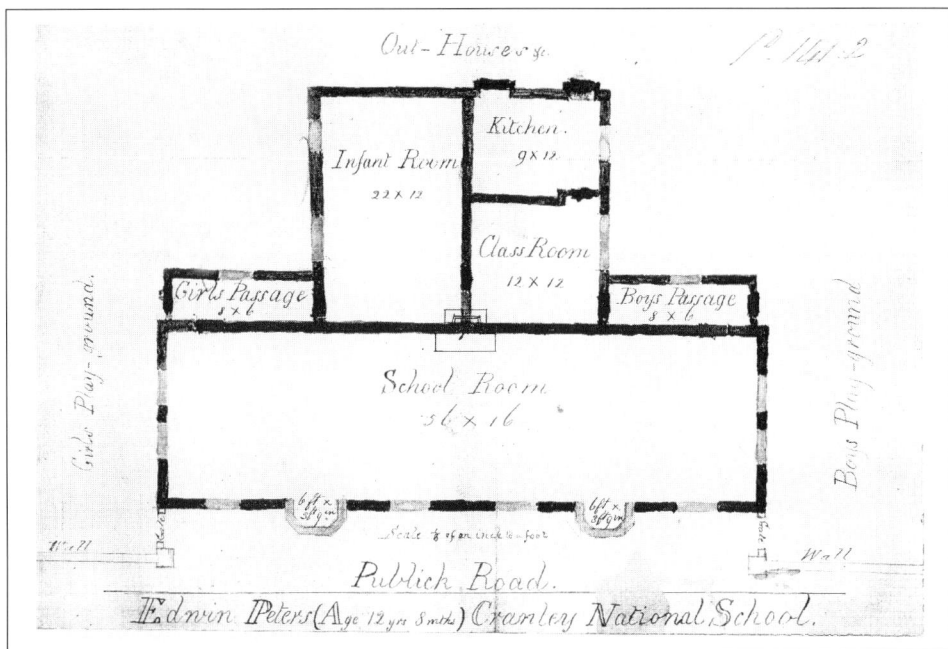

19. Edwin Peters' Plan of Cranley National School, 1853
[Copyright of Surrey History Service]

A second Admissions Register lists those registered between 1848 and 1871; rather confusingly it also lists some of the entries back to 1848, presumably copied from the first register. In this, the first of only four 1848 entries is Ellen Stemp, who as a result has, in several publications, been wrongly listed as the first to be registered. Ellen was registered on March 7th as aged six, living on Cranley Common, with a father who was a Labourer. [10] One wonders what relation Ellen was to the striking figure of the Mr Stemp who, with a youngster named Tom Smallpiece, adorns a wonderful old photograph in 'Bygone Cranleigh'. [11]

The twenty pupils admitted in 1850 included the children of Mr Ede the village innkeeper, Mr Pullen the grocer, Mr Parsons the carpenter, and Mr Peters the blacksmith. In 1853 thirty-five new pupils were admitted, to make the total over one hundred. The names of Steadman, Parsons, Carpenter and Tickner reappear constantly in the registers. The majority of the fathers were labourers. Every pupil came from some part of Cranley except a Matilda Luck, whose permanent residence was in London, her father being a waterman. There was a link with the Wey and Arun canal as two fathers' residences were recorded as being at the Bridge; their occupations were 'wharfingers'. Ann Manfield's father was a brickmaker, and their residence was 'Cranley Brickyard'. A schoolmaster at Dunsfold sent his daughter to the school in 1857. A printer is recorded as living in Cranley in 1858, and another one in the following year. The word 'Tradesman' appeared for the first time in this year, and one parent was a nurse - the village hospital had recently opened. 1860 recorded the daughters of a London coachman and a photographer from Bagshot, and the following year a police constable's daughter from Normandy was entered. Gradually, therefore, children came from further afield; maybe some had moved temporarily to Cranley while their fathers were on particular jobs.

At first few children had had previous instruction. William Knight, son of the village carrier, was an exception: he had been taught until he was seven by a Miss Emma Crewdson, who was the daughter of Richard Crewdson, the contractor for the National School. But during the 1860s 'Cranley Nursery School' and 'Gray's Wood Nursery School' are mentioned, and also a chapel school. [12]

Log Books

From 1863 schools were required to keep a daily record of activities in log books. During the first days of term more children were admitted in ones and twos, and the Curate was recorded as taking two classes a week. Bad weather prevented the children coming to school on several occasions as these entries show:

May 15th.	This day 30 per cent absent.
May 19th.	Owing to very heavy rain 50 per cent absent.
May 20th.	Very wet, 56 per cent absent.

The Rector and the Curate both came in several times to take classes. No slackness was allowed:

June 10th.   Warning given to George Charman (1st. class) for repeated neglect of home lessons.

The school children attended church at least once a week, sometimes having a scripture class and attending church on the same day. Some examinations set by Her Majesty's Inspectors were given to the children in various subjects:

June 25th.	Examined fourth in Reading and Dictation. Fair.
June 30th.	Examined third in Arithmetic. Moderate.
July 2nd.	Examined second in Dictation. Moderate.

There were also some curious entries - for example:

June 13th. W. Fuller swallowed a piece of slate pencil. No harm resulted.

From August 3rd to September 5th there were school holidays called 'Harvest Vacation'. At the beginning of the Autumn Term more children were admitted, and a school feast or harvest thanksgiving occurred:

Sept. 10th. School Feast - about 170 children, present and past scholars. Holiday service at church at 5p.m. as a conclusion and harvest thanks-giving.

Numbers rose steadily during this term and November 23rd began the week with an attendance of 102. The November 25th entry is:

First Stone of Surrey County School [now Cranleigh School] laid by the Archbishop of Canterbury assisted by the Bishop of Winchester and the Rector of Cranley - Elder children to be present, no school pm.

The Rector was one of the original Governors of the Surrey County School; indeed, it had been a conversation he had had in 1862 with the local M.P., the Rt. Hon. G. Cubitt, which had led directly to this school's foundation, 'for the sons of farmers, traders and the professions'. [13]

The Log Book reveals that in December night lessons were held, and the holidays did not begin until Christmas Eve. A Christmas present of clothes was given to those children who had attended most regularly from the date of their admission:

December 24th. Ten girls presented with new frocks. Eleven boys present-ed with warm cloth capes at an expense of £5, which sum was given to the Rector by a lady to be expended as he thought best.

There are two entries in the Log Book concerning 1864 that are worth quot-ing. The first, for July 27th, details the Report of HM Inspector of Cranley National School, and is signed by 'J.H. Sapte, Manager and Rector':

Cranley N.S.

Mixed - The school is not in a satisfactory condition. The arithmetic seems to have been neglected and the Dictation was badly done. More desks are necessary and the offices require alteration. The Needlework done in my presence was only moderate, even making allowance for the youth of the children.

Night - The Night School is held in the same room as the Day School and appears to be productive of great good among the heretofore ignorant rustics of Cranley.

My visit unfortunately took place at a time when very few scholars could attend as it was during the hay season, on a very wet night, and the day after the annual Cranley Feast. Those who came however acquitted themselves in such a manner as to show that very good gains had been taken with their instruction.

So by 1865 the School, after 18 years, was well established if not free of problems. The next Head Teacher was to oversee its first major extensions.

THOMAS MOUSLEY(1865-80)

In 1865 the Poores were succeeded by Mr. and Mrs. Thomas Mousley. Attendance details for one week in June, 1868, were:

	Number on register	School fees received
Class I:	28	1s 9d
Class II:	21	2s 0d
Class III:	27	1s 11d
Class IV:	36	3s 0d
Class V:	45	3s 6d
Total	157	12s 2d

Average number present: 114. [14]

Major Extensions

No doubt in response to the Education Act of 1870, the first plans to add East and West wings to the National School building were submitted on 23 September 1870. Archdeacon Sapte gave the site and an appeal was sent out to the 'landed proprietors'.The major contributor was Mr. Thurlow of Baynards Park. The stone was given by the owners of Knowle and again carted free of charge by the local farmers. [15]

The plans for the extensions had been revised in March 1871; the West Wing became a 'Boys School for 59' and the East Wing an 'Infant School for 100'. Log book entries reveal that, after numerous delays, the infants first used their new room on 28 October 1872, and on the following day 'the Upper School' were taught in theirs for the first time. [16] Between the Wings each had their own playgrounds and in the north part of the original building, between the playgrounds, were lavatories. The original school room, by the road, was now unevenly divided into a 'Boys Class Room for 24' and a 'Girls School for 67'. To the north of the whole building were separate playgrounds for Elder Boys and for Girls. [17]

Homes and Occupations

Kept at St. Nicolas School are nine books each titled 'Register of Admission, Progress and Withdrawal' for Cranleigh National School. The first, covering the years 1872 to 78, begins:

Principal Teacher: Thos H. Mousley   2nd class
Date of taking charge: 65(Y) 9(M)

Assistant Teacher: Frances Warren   Ex. P.T.

1872 Certificated 3rd Div. 1st Yr.
Date of entering on Situation: 71(Y) 2(M)

Pupil Teachers:-
John Stemp, b. 23 Apr. 1859
Date of Apprenticeship: 73(Y) 6(M)
Date of Leaving: 77(Y) 5(M)

Matilda Lufkin, b. 22 Mar. 1860
Date of Apprenticeship: 74(Y) 6(M)'

The first page of the Pupil Register of 1872 (see overleaf) lists 36 boys and girls. Four were aged 3, eleven 4, seven 5, four 6, three 7, one 8, three 11, one 12, one 13, and one 14. Six of them are listed as living on Cranleigh Common, three at each of Bookhurst and Nanhurst, two at each of Wildwood, Wickles, Smithwood Common, Station Yard, Pass Bridge, and Village, and one at each of Parkhatch, Cranleigh, Knowle Lodge, Gt. Gasson, Wanborough, Hollyhock, Railway Station, Crow Lane, Baynards, Clapper Bridge, Nethersall and Colmans. Where on earth, a modern resident would ask, are some of these now?

Under 'Occupation of parent' there are listed 26 Labourers, 3 Plate Layers, 2 Blacksmiths, 1 Shoemaker, 1 Groom, 1 Gardener, 1 Station Master and 1 Publican. On other pages are listed many other occupations: Builder, Widow, Painter, Carter, Railway Porter, Glazier, Plumber, Tailor, Clothier, illegitimate, Wheelwright, Miller, Shepherd, Farm Bailiff, Station clerk, Bricklayer, Carpenter, Timber Dealer, Harness-maker, Baker, Drill Sergeant, Servant, Charwoman, Cordwainer, Surveyor, Orphan, Brickmaker, Brickmaker Foreman, Brickyard Manager, Police Sergeant, Coachman, House Decorator, Butler, Seedsman, Grocer, Woodman, Mechanic Carrier, Yeoman, Keeper, Wharfinger, Waterman, Shopkeeper, Inspector of Police, Photographer, Platelayer, Coachman, Schoolmaster, Stonemason, Patient (leg off!), Plasterer, Beer-Shopkeeper, Clergyman, Farrier, Pensioner, Hawker, Shoemaker, Navvy, Printer, Carrier and Farmer. [18]

Admission Number 1872	Name of Child	Age Y M	Admission to the School Y M	Residence	Occupation of Parent
Brot. from Old 73R		16 16			
872. 32	Dicker Catherine	5 6	72 2	Wookhurst	Shoemaker
873. 33	Colwrich, Henry	4 7	74 9	Parkhatch	Laborer
874. 34	Hottridge Elizabeth	3 5	72 2	Cranleigh	Groom &c
875. 35	Stamps Frank	4 5	72 2	Knowle Lodge	Gardener
876. 36	Trigden Walter A.	7	74 2	Cranleigh Comn	Blacksmith
877. 37	Tanner William	4	72 3	St. Casson	Laborer
878. 38	Street Solomon	6 2	72 3	Wookhurst	Laborer
879. 39	Mercer James	4 1	72 3	Brookhurst	Laborer
880. 40	Harkes Edith	4 10	72 3	The Common	Laborer
881. 41	Ansell Mark	4	72 3	Wanborough	Laborer
882. 42	Woolgar Emma	5 7	72 4	Hollyhock	Laborer
883. 43	Sandford Alice	5 5	72 4	Nanhurst	Laborer
884. 44	Sandford Mary	7 8	72 4	"	"
885. 45	Sandford Sarah	11	72 4	"	"
886. 46	Frances Emily	12 3	72 4	Wildwood	Labourer
887. 47	Leale Margaret	3	72 4	Railway Stn	Station Master
888. 48	Trusler Emily	6	72 4	Nickles	Labourer
889. 49	Maidwell William	5 3	72 4	Crow Lane	Labourer
890. 50	Stamps Esther	4 11	72 4	Smithwood Comn	Labourer
891. 51	Neale William	6 4	72 4	Maynards	Labourer
892. 52	Perry Alice	11 7	72 4	Cranleigh Comn	Laborer
893. 52	Perry James	5	72 4	"	"
894. 53	Perry Albert	3 8	72 4	"	"
895. 54	Bennett Alfred	4 8	72 4	Smithwood	Laborer
896. 55	Dowding Ellen	11 1	72 4	Clapper Bridge	Laborer
897. 56	Horsfold James		72 4	Wildwood	Labourer
898. 57	Trusler Sarah A.	14	72 4	Nickles	Laborer
899. 58	Hottington Emma	13 8	72 5	Station Yard	Ry. Plate Layer
900. 59	Whittington Alfd	7 4	72 5	"	"
901. 60	Whittington Walter	5 7	72 5	Common	
902. 61	Charman Emma	5 1	72 5		
903. 62	Boxall Alice	8	72 5	Pass Bridge	Laborer
904. 63	Tatter James	3	72 5	Village	Blacksmith
905. 64	Francis, Mary Ann	6 3	72 5	Wethersell Hills	Labourer
906. 65	Mercer James	3	72 5	Village	Publican
907. 66	Segram Emily Anna	7 5	72 5	Pass Bridge	Laborer
908. 68	Shullock Lucy	4 7	72 4	Common	Laborer
71-1872. Admitted B.32 G 36					

20. *Extract from 1872 register of Cranleigh National School*
[Copyright of Surrey History Service]

What a wonderful microcosm of Victorian Cranleigh life! A clear indication that Cranleigh's compact farming community was being enriched by a variety of skilled trades.

Inspector's Report

In October 1873 there were reports of the growth of the school and of the advantages of the extensions:

> Inspector's Report. The school has much increased in number since its removal to the new schoolroom. In attainments an advance has been reached, especially in the Reading of the upper Standards. In elementary attainments the girls are behind the boys in consequence of the afternoons being all of them devoted to needlework. The infants in the new schoolroom are in nice order and under careful instruction. [19]

Whereas in 1848 it had cost £88 to run the school for one year, in 1875 it cost £248.10s.6d. This sum included payment for an Infant School Mistress (£43.3s.4d.), a Pupil Teacher (£22.15s.0d.), and Insurance (10s.). The appointment of an Infant School Mistress allowed children below the age of six to be in a separate class. By now the school was no longer supported solely by the clergy and wealthy parishioners; the Reverend Sapte and Mr. Bradshaw now needed to give only £5 each. [20]

In September 1878 there was more trouble over school attendance:

> Edward Steadman, 2nd Standard, has not yet returned to school being at times very irregular, the case was brought under the notice of the school attendance officer.

Cranleigh, being without a school board, was obliged to have a school attendance officer after 1876.

In October 1878 there was confusion over the admission of an orphan:

> Difficulty experienced in respect to the admission of Freda Reed an orphan. The street and district in London being unknown. The certificate of birth cannot be traced. [21]

The School was now over 40 years old, and there was soon to be another change of Head.

21. *Henry Hayman in 1919*
(Headmaster 1880 to 1920)
[Blogg papers]

HENRY HAYMAN (1880-1920)

In 1880 Mr. Henry J. Hayman, a young man in his mid-twenties, born in Ewhurst, took over as Head Teacher from Thomas Mousley.

Log book entries comment on a variety of issues. [22] In November 1882 there was a widespread epidemic and much absence. The medical officer reported: 'I should consider it very imprudent to compel parents to send their children to Cranleigh National School during the present epidemic.' On November 13th the medical officer closed the school for a fortnight and ordered it to be thoroughly disinfected with fluid and sulphur.

There were 225 pupils on the books in 1883 (including the Infant School), but on July 30th the log book records: 'Today I have sent a list of absentees to the Attendance Officer: 60 names'. Mr. Hayman's subtle response is recorded in the log book on November 29th: 'I have asked the Rector to have a scheme by which every child present punctually .... each week will receive a halfpenny for every such week, at the end of the school year. He has thought the matter over and is now willing to give it a trial'. The Rector duly published a notice announcing that 'at the end of the School year, May

31st 1884... a Child present punctually and regularly in School for Twenty-four weeks, would be entitled to One Shilling'. The log book entry for Monday, 3 December 1883 reads: 'Many more children present today'. Regular attendance was soon up to 81%. This was important, among other reasons, because grants were linked to attendance as well as to proficiency in certain subjects. In 1884, for example, the school's grant was £160.16s.0d., with a small sum allotted to each subject.

Health

Deficiences both of intelligence and of health are very evident from Mr. Hayman's entry dated April 27th, 1885:

Emily Channon who is mentioned as a delicate child (Feb 3) is now dead.

Children to be excused from Exam in June:

Ellen Jenner	defective intellect
Annie Shrub	Imbecile
Mary Shrub	Imbecile
Lassam Alice	delicate, consumptive child
Beadell	Request of parents on account of danger of Brain Disease
Tarm Walter	Delicate
Parsons Ellen	Deaf at times
Moore Annie	Bad eyes

The Inspector's Report on the School in 1885 refers to a matter which may have played its own part in the health issue: 'I find that notwithstanding last year's caution, the main schoolroom has been washed only once, the classroom but twice. I must again urge that all floors should be washed not less than every two months, for the sake of purity of atmosphere and general cleanliness'.

The 1890s

The Admissions Register 1893-1906 contains a revealing variety of 'Causes of leaving the school', which often refers to jobs undertaken. The commonest entries are 'gone away' and 'transferred'. Some of the others are: age, to service, to private school, hospital, has fits, fever, weak eyes, broken arm, ill, deceased, measles - left almost blind on recovery, scholarship, work as brewery boy or plumber's boy or dressmaking or farming or house boy, to help mother, to orphan school, dairy work, brick making, work in garden, errand boy for greengrocer, telegraph boy, cycle trade, brickyard, monitress, domestic service, butcher's boy, brewery office, errand boy for dairy, draper's boy, pageboy, nurse girl, and private study. [23]

22. Fifty Years of Progress: 1905
[Blogg papers]

23. The original Infants School in 1908
[Blogg papers]

In 1894 Archdeacon Sapte was largely instrumental in having a large room for infants built on the north side of the existing buildings, carefully planned to receive the best light. This room is shown in a plan of the time [24], and it is mentioned in a Surveyor's Report dated 1905 and will soon be referred to again. [25]

A log book entry for January 1896, by which time there were 267 children on the books, shows the school timetable of that date. Subjects mentioned include Writing and Reading, Arithmetic, Geography, Occupations, Drawing Maps, Grammar, History, Singing, and Playground school drill. [26]

A new building for Infants

Cranleigh's population in 1901 had risen to 2,709. By 1904 the National School was so overcrowded that the infants were moved into the village hall. The Managers of the Church of England Schools had not the money for further extensions, but in 1906 an entirely new building was erected by the Surrey County Council to the east of the Church on the site of two fields given in the previous year by William Welch. The urgent need for the 1906 building was highlighted in the 1905 Surveyor's Report which stressed the limitations of the classrooms in the buildings of 1847 and 1871. 'The buildings are very awkwardly arranged', it says, and then:

Classroom 'A': This is a long narrow room too big for one class and too small for two. [Ditto for Classroom 'D'].

Classroom 'B': A very poor, narrow, low room. [Ditto for Classroom 'C'].

Infants Main Room: An excellent modern room but too large to be without divisions.

Two very limited playgrounds: one for boys and one for girls and infants.

There is other information in the Report, as follows:

Number of Teachers: Male - 3 for Infants. Female - 4 for the Mixed School, 3 for the Infants School

Children under 8 conveyed from Smithwood Common & Hazlewood during winter. Children from Baynards by train. Children from Winterfold, private conveyance by Lord Alverstone. [27]

Punishments

One of the most revealing of the documents kept at St Nicolas Junior School is a Punishment Book which has entries from 1909 to 1925 and then from 1944 to 1960. Here are seven examples from the earlier dates:

1910	writing notes with improper phrases (four stripes on hand)
	passing the above (two stripes on hand)
1910	caught stealing boy's dinner (caned)
1910	attempted to bite teacher (caned)
1915	telling his parents lies about his treatment at school and writing to his mother and saying the note was from me (caned)
1917	applying brake to tractor and compelling driver to stop engine (caned 1 stripe)
1920	making a stupid joke during 2 minutes silence (caned 3 stripes on hand, 4 across buttocks, punishment in front of class). [28]

War

To mark the opening of the renovated Arts Centre in 1998, a Glebelands School play recorded events in the history of the village school. One scene reported that by November 27th, 1914, some 1,100 soldiers were billetted in the village, and that several of the older girls were allowed to come to school late so that they could help their mothers provide the soldiery with breakfast. It also reminded us that the war 'cost the lives of 118 of the fathers, grandfathers, brothers and cousins of the kids of Cranleigh'. [29]

In 1920 Mr. Hayman retired as Head Teacher. He had once said: 'I was always concerned to see to it that the young people who left our school were in possession of good manners and a strong belief in the Word of God'. He seems to have succeeded, at least to some extent, if a local guide book printed some ten years later is to be believed: 'After 39 years service to the children of Cranleigh, during which time he won the hearts of all whom he taught, and by his example and precepts raised the tone of Cranleigh child-life to a high standard, he retired'. [30] What teacher would not like to have that written about him or her?

FRANK ENGLISH (1920-42)

Mr. Frank English succeeded Mr. Hayman. About 300 pupils attended the school at this time, with a staff of eight teachers. The County School for Infants had about 200 children. Sometime, it seems between 1910 and 1924, the older of the schools became known as The Church of England Junior School rather than the National School.

The older school's Punishment Book has what turns out to be a remarkable final entry in 1925: 'Use of cane to be discontinued. This was the unanimous decision of the staff after a lengthy discussion as to the effectiveness of corporal punishment'. No further canings, or indeed punishments of any sort, are recorded until 1942, when Mr. English was succeeded by Mr. Blogg and corporal punishment is again referred to. [31]

But it is clear that the 1925 entry gives a quite false impression, because

Mr. Vic Philpot, for one, had personal experience of Mr. English and is certain that caning did not stop. Mr. Philpot, now a sprightly 82, went to the school in 1924 at the age of seven. In 1930 he won a scholarship to Guildford Junior Technical School - seven out of twenty-one in the top class, Standard 7, were given a scholarship each year. Vic served in the 1939-45 war, after which a friend convinced him that he should apply for the one-year emergency teacher-training scheme in London: 'I always wanted to be a teacher, but in the 1930s there was no way my parents could afford the training'. In 1947 he began teaching at his old school, and later became Headmaster of Ewhurst School in 1960 and then of Park Mead Junior School from 1968 to 1981.

But we must go back to 1929 and an English lesson which Mr. English was teaching to Standard 6, which included Vic. This episode made a splendid scene in the Glebelands School's play, for which Vic supplied the detail.

Mr. English asked the pupils how to spell 'crozier'. Many children got it wrong - all were ordered to the front. Finally Vic (secretly, he confesses, with the aid of a dictionary) got it right. Mr. English said to him: 'Philpot, fetch my cane from my office. The scholars at the front will be punished for their ignorance. Hold out your hands!' [32]

24. *Cranleigh C. of E. school performance of Scenes from 'Twelfth Night' at the Rectory Fête, 1927*
[Blogg papers]

The children performed 'Twelfth Night' at the Rectory Fête of 1926. Their performances raised £19 towards the £112 required for a folding wood and glass screen for the large north room of the school. The parish magazine reported: 'The entertainment of July 7th was the effort of staff and children for their own school. And a capital effort it was! The part-songs and the country dances were performed with a naturalness which showed not only good training, but that kind of training which sets free rather than hampers the natural gift. The children were evidently enjoying themselves as well as giving enjoyment to others'. [33]

Inspection

The 1935 Inspection Report was clearly not to the Headmaster's liking. Mr. English makes this all too clear in the log book:

> The following report was received on resumption of school but as I considered it unjust I refused to enter it until after consultation with the County Inspector which took place on Oct. 22nd.

> 'This county school is situated in one of the most beautiful Surrey villages on the edge of the North Downs. It serves the village of Cranleigh and a scattered rural community within a radius of three miles and contains 264 children taught in six classes by the Head Master, four certificated and two uncertificated teachers with the part-time assistance of Instructors in Woodwork, Gardening and Domestic Subjects. The School is a pleasant and happy place: the relationship between teachers and their pupils is good throughout and a praiseworthy and successful effort is made to train the children in good habits and to inculcate pride both in themselves and in the school. The actual achievements of the children do not, however, give equal cause for satisfaction. This is due to the fact that the Headmaster has not grasped the possibilities of organisation and chiefly development in a rural school containing such a large number of senior scholars. The schemes of work do not involve any research, very few notes are made, reference books are rarely consulted by the children themselves and the oral lessons, though on the whole not lacking in substance, need clearer objectives in order to secure more individual effort from the children.

> A good start is made in the two lowest classes where the vitality of the teaching and consequent alertness of the children were clearly evident.

> The Headmaster has in his staff teachers of varied talents. He would be wise to reconsider his schemes having full regard to the teaching power available and by widening the scope of the work, thereby stimulating the children to greater effort'. [34]

It is obvious why the Head was not too happy, and one wonders what, if anything, he persuaded the Inspector to alter.

Empire Day and War

Empire Day still continued to be an important annual celebration, though not, of course, for very much longer. Pupils were regaled with detail of the glory of the Empire, and Vic Philpot particularly remembers singing 'Flag of Britain proudly waving' and 'Land of our Birth we pledge to Thee'. The Empire was soon to be embroiled in another war which was to add pupils to the village school in a way that was far from ideal.

Threat of German bombing in 1939 brought young evacuees from London, with their identification ribbons and labels, their baggage and their gas-mask boxes. They assembled in the Lady Peek Institute by the church until they were found homes. The organization was masterminded by a worthy but rather stressed Cranleigh gentleman, one of whose remarks circulated in the village for some time thereafter. Forcibly disclaiming accountability for certain adults who had been evacuated with the children he shouted, 'I am NOT responsible for all these pregnant women!' [35]

Some of the evacuee children were taught in the school building, others in the village hall, others elsewhere. Life in the school became harder as some of the teachers were called up or transferred, and as epidemics of chicken-pox and measles hit the pupils. When these opening months turned out to be a 'phoney war' some of the evacuees returned to London, but later in 1942 a second group arrived from St. Peter's School, Wapping, in the East End.

In the middle year of the War Mr. English's twenty-two years as Head came to an end.

CLAUDE BLOGG (1942-67)

In August 1942 Mr. Claude Blogg became Headmaster. Much about his time as Head can be found in his own papers. He had previously been an Assistant Master for about ten years before the War, and had then for several years been Headmaster in Shere.

Flying Bomb

One of the first things he did was to inspect the air-raid shelters, which he found 'in a disgraceful condition' and which he soon had cleaned up. Contemporaries remember him striding through the village keeping an eye on scattered classes as he sought to cope with the evacuees, but there was nothing he could do to prevent the events of the day in 1944 which he recorded in this Log Book entry: 'School closed owing to extensive damage due to Flying Bomb which demolished the Infants School at 7a.m. on Sunday August 27th'. [36]

25. Cranleigh Infant School destroyed by Flying Bomb, 7 a.m. Sunday, 24 August 1944
[Blogg papers]

A fuller précis of the events of the day begins:

> On Sunday Aug. 27th 1944 at 7 a.m. a flying bomb dropped in the playground of the Council Infants School destroying that school and the adjacent Practical Instruction Centre of the Cranleigh C. of E. School. The C. of E. School itself which is some 100 yds from where the bomb exploded suffered serious damage being rendered throughout unusable. Mercifully there was no one on the premises of either school. The chairman of the C. of E. School, the Revd. H. L. Johnston, who was in his rectory grounds when the bomb fell, was the only casuality, he being removed to hospital with head injury from blast and falling tiles. Faced with the task of carrying on the education of some 500 children attending the two schools with the minimum of delay the Managers took steps to seek and inspect all available accommodation in the neighbourhood. The Village Hall, the Methodist Church room, St. Andrew's Church room and later a room of the British Legion were secured by agreement and, after a break of only two days, education was recommenced on Wednesday Aug.30th for 224 senior children (Stds III to VII) of the C.of E. School of whom 191 (85%) attended on the first day. [37]

As for the infants, a temporary school, built of wood, was put up to house them. This still stands alongside the later, more modern, buildings.

Pupil Recollections

Ruth Denyer (later Mrs. Heather), a pupil at the School from 1936 to 1943 recollects:

'My first headmaster was Mr. English and then Mr. Blogg. Other teachers were Miss Martin, Mr. Johns, Mr. Peak, Mr. Milner (who was a very interesting teacher), Mr. Gwillam, Mrs. Bathurst, Mrs. Aldridge and Miss O'Kane. The Headmaster's office was in an upstairs room in the Lady Peek Institute. Also in the Institute buns were sold to the children at break times. These were supplied by Hibbs bakers and sold by Mr. and Mrs. Streeter.

Domestic science was taught by Miss O'Kane in a building in a corner of the playground of the first school. There was one large room where the girls were taught cooking, washing, ironing etc. and a smaller room had a bed where the girls were taught how to make the bed and polish the floor. The boys had a small part of the large room for woodwork. Rev. Hugh Johnston was rector and went into the school regularly. Mr. Blogg taught most of the Religious Education and the Lord's Prayer, Catechism and Nicene Creed had to be learnt by every child. Because Mr. Blogg was so enthusiastic, hymns were known inside out and backwards!

Every Ascension Day Rev. Hugh Johnston gave the children a small Bible (donated by the Peacock Trust). Mr. Hayman presented prayer books to the school for each child.

The school had a sandstone wall around it, running from the front by the main road, down the side to the back. This had two gates - one in the side and one at the back. Outside the wall were two playgrounds, one at the back which was tarmaced and the boys used, and a rough one at the side for the girls.

Milk was given to each child at morning break. It was kept in the hearth by an open fire which made it taste awful!'

Marjorie Charman (later Mrs. White), at the school from 1939 to 1946, wrote:

'We had reason as a family to be grateful for the sound basic education we received at Cranleigh C of E.

Whenever there was a funeral in the church and we were at play we all stood to attention and bowed our heads. At times of an air-raid we all walked in orderly crocodiles to the shelters which were in a field beyond the church [in the grounds of the present St. Nicolas School]; very often the all-clear sounded before we had time to reach the shelters but if not we sat in them reciting our times table or singing - depending on the teacher's mood.

On Ascension Day we always walked via Winterfold to St James' Seat where the rector [the Rev. Hugh Johnston] conducted a short service. We then had a picnic and games in the car park at the bottom of Pitch Hill before walking back. We were amazed when the London children joined us but came by coach.

Promotion from classes was mainly by merit, although I cannot recall anyone being held back for years and years. I loved reading but class reading books were scarce and I remember the disappointment of silent reading sessions at Christmas when the choice was either "The Snow Queen" or "The Water Babies". I felt I knew them by heart!

There was no school uniform and I can remember feeling immensely proud when my brother went to Guildford and wore a cap with a red quarter at the front and later when I had a blue blazer for school. Mr. Blogg came to Cranleigh from Shere where they had a thriving stoolball club; he introduced it to Cranleigh and for matches we would cycle over the hills to Shere, play, and then cycle back.

Our house was damaged when a doodlebug hit the gasometer close to the bottom of our garden. My mother was getting tea at the time. We heard the engine cut out and she tried to pull me into the cupboard under the stairs but I preferred to take cover under the table as there were spiders in the cupboard!'

Ruth Denyer's daughter, Susan (later Mrs. Ansell), was a pupil from 1958 to 1962. She recalls:

'Once a year we competed in the Godalming and District School Sports. These were always held at Godalming (don't remember where) and the school always came back with one or more cups.

We always took part in a short play at the Rectory Fete. I was one of the children in the Pied Piper of Hamlyn one year.

Every Christmas the school put on concerts in the village hall. Each class did a sketch. I was in Dick Whittington one year.

During breaks some children would sneak across to the Dairy in the Ewhurst Road (where the Surrey Advertiser office is now) to buy sweets. This was forbidden and if caught the child would be punished with lines (a hundred, I think)'. [38]

Discipline

This seems a good cue to quote a few more entries from the official Punishment Book:

1944   fooling about in Church during special morning prayers for our Invasion Forces (1 stripe with cane)

1952	stole rolls from Hibbs (two strokes with the cane)
1955	painting another boy's face (one stroke on each hand)
1959	played truant - went off to Vachery Pond to sail boat (caned on hands)
1960	poured practically whole tin of fish food into Class 4 Fish Tank - all died (a thorough smacking) [39]

Discipline cannot have been helped by the size of the classes. Vic Philpot recalled: 'One year I had 50 in my class - 45 was common'.

Secondary Schooling

The minutes of a meeting of the School Managing Body in March 1946 refer to its 'grave concern at the lack of secondary education for the children of Cranleigh'. [40] Eventually Mr Blogg, in his December 16th prizegiving review of 1948, was able to announce that:

'1948 will be remembered by us all as the year when at last a great educational step was taken in Cranleigh. I refer, of course, to the opening of the hutted school at the back of The Greyhound. [These huts had been erected by German prisoners-of-war.] The valuable equipment which the Authority has provided is a wonderful advance on what was thought necessary for primary school children before the war.

Educational experts tell us that only about 10% of the child population of this country is really fitted for the bookish-type of secondary education. Although I am delighted when children have the good fortune to win awards qualifying them to go to Grammar Schools in Guildford and elsewhere, the teachers and I have always felt sorry for the children left behind, for whom, up to the present, little or no improved form of education has been possible.

The hutted school will give us at last a fine opportunity of developing a new form of secondary work of a more practical type, and which in the long run will be very much better suited to our boys and girls...When school reopened after the summer holidays on August 31st....71 children from Ewhurst, Ellens Green, Alfold, Dunsfold and Grafham, and 86 children from our own school in Cranleigh , all $12\frac{1}{2}$ years and over, were transferred to the hutted department'.

Exam Successes

In his review Mr. Blogg also reported on academic and other honours:

'On February 12th this year 27 children who passed the preliminary of the Common Entrance Exam. took the final test in Guildford. We are pleased and proud to tell you that five boys gained awards to the Royal Grammar

School, five girls to the Guildford County School, two boys to the Pewley County Secondary School, Guildford, and one girl won an award to the Godalming Grammar School, making a total of 13 awards.

During the year two girls won awards to the Guildford Commercial School; one girl won an award to the Guildford School of Art; one boy, Robert Cross, won an award to the Guildford Technical School.

From an examination point of view 1948, therefore, has been a very successful year indeed.

I am very pleased to tell you that no fewer than six of the scholarship winners from our school since 1942 have gained their School Leaving Cerificate, five of them have Matriculated, which means they fully justified their opportunity of receiving a Grammar School education.

Last summer term Marjorie Charman was head girl of the Guildford Commercial School, and another old C. of E. scholar, Gilbert Renaud, was head boy of the Guildford Technical School. An honour and credit to the young people concerned and an honour to Cranleigh.

We again entered the Godalming and District School Sports on June 2nd, and scored 74 points, the most we have ever gained in this competition.' [41]

Glebelands

Until 1956 the secondary pupils being taught in the Horsa huts continued to form part of the Church of England School. But in that year, with the Church unable to raise the money to build a new secondary school, the County Authority took control of the 'huts department' and a separate Headmaster, Mr. John Wiskar, was appointed. Other classrooms were added on the north side of Parsonage Road, and this all became a Secondary Modern School called The County Secondary School.

In November 1956 construction of the new buildings began. These were completed at the end of 1958, at which time the name 'Glebelands County Secondary School' was first used. John Wiskar wrote: 'By 1960 our numbers will be nearer 500 than 400. The staff by January 1959 will number 17.' The main buildings were officially opened in July 1959.

Plans to move

Meanwhile the Church of England Junior School continued as such, though with numbers growing the need for a new site became ever-greater. This was highlighted in some detail in the log book entry for November 14th, 1961, which outlines the opinion of the Inspector:

> This voluntary school was built in 1847. For over a century it has served this community, first as an all-age school and since 1956 as a Junior

School....in many respects it fails to reach the minimum standards of building provision that are now acceptable....altogether about one third of an acre....very small playground....two of the six classes seriously overcrowded....in two classes natural lighting poor....no supply of hot water....WCs insufficient for the 237 pupils on the roll....the staff use outdoor WCs....a wide spread of ability and this is particularly marked in reading....the problem of teaching pupils to spell correctly has not been solved....disappointing standard of writing....a happy school....possibilities for further development, which has not yet been fully realised, are challenging. [42]

So it was the 1961 report which led directly to plans for a move to new buildings. Of the total cost of £70,000, the School Managers were required to raise over £15,500. Fund-raising began.There were open days, exhibitions of work, Christmas concerts, jumble sales, and in 1965 the Rectory Fete raised a record £541.8s.7d.

To Parsonage Road

On Midsummer Day, 24th June, in 1966, the pupils moved from the buildings that had housed Cranleigh children for 119 years. They moved to new buildings in Parsonage Road. The school's log book entry for 22nd October is:

Dedication and Opening of the New School Building in Parsonage Road. (Lady Thatcher attended.) Just before the service began John Tallon (Head Boy) rang the old 1848 School Bell which had been brought from the old building in Cranleigh High Street.

The new buildings were designed to take 280 children. The Horsa huts, now free of secondary students, housed a further 50 children. They are still in use today.

The following year Mr. Blogg retired after 25 years as Head. A plaque in the present Arts Centre reads: 'Claude E. Blogg: Assistant and Headmaster for 34 years: A lifetime of service'.

FROM 1967 TO 1998

Since Mr. Blogg's retirement in 1967, the Headteachers of the Church of England School have been:

September 1967	Peter Corbett
January 1978	David Simmons
April 1986	David Ellerington
September 1988	Ann Keig
September 1998	John Reading

26. Mr. Blogg and children as St. Nicolas School is built (c.1965)
[Blogg papers]

On 10th September 1973 the log book records the change of the school's name to Cranleigh Church of England Middle School. 'This new school opened today. On the roll there were 560 children. Over 300 of these children are transported on school coaches.' [43]

In 1990 the school was renamed again, and became what it now is: St. Nicolas School. The name appropriately reflects the close ties with the Parish Church that have existed since 1847. On 7th June 1997, a Pageant Fayre was held at St. Nicolas School to celebrate its 150th Anniversary. The programme recalled '150 very exciting years'.[44]

'We try to make children's lives extraordinary,' writes the present Head, Mr. John Reading in his school's prospectus. No longer are there references, as in the 1864 Inspector's Report, to 'the ignorant rustics of Cranley'. The future looks good.

CHAPTER 5

THE HOSPITAL

27. *The Cranleigh Village Hospital in 1902*

Cranleigh Village Hospital opened its doors for patients in October 1859. There is an interesting story which may well be the birth of the idea of having a hospital in Cranleigh. It seems that the Rector was out riding one morning when he was told of a severe accident, the victim having been taken to a nearby cottage. On going there to see what help he might be able to give, he found Dr. Napper, the local doctor, and the village policeman about to amputate the poor man's leg. The local druggist who was to have been the anaesthetist had fainted and was useless. This occurrence impressed itself on the minds of both men so that the idea of a hospital took shape.

Dr. Napper was a local man by birth and came from a family that had lived in this area of Surrey and Sussex for many years: the first recorded Napper being in 1404 in the reign of Henry IV, the name probably arising from the trade of flint-napping in the Weald of Sussex. Dr. Albert Napper was a well qualified and respected surgeon who had walked the wards at St.Thomas' Hospital before qualifying for his degree; he spent a year in Edinburgh, then, as now, renowned for its medical teaching. He went to Germany to study for two years, then in 1848 started a medical practice in Guildford.

In 1854 he acquired the Cranleigh practice which is when he met and became friendly with the Rector, John Sapte.

The Rector provided the cottage opposite the church (believed to have been the priest's dwelling in the Middle Ages) which still exists and is the nucleus of the present hospital. The cottage, which, according to a survey made some years ago still has woodwork dating from over 400 years ago, was leased by the Rector to the hospital at a rental of £5 per annum which he returned as a donation. Dr. Napper was the Medical Officer and the Archdeacon was the Manager with Napper definitely in charge of the hospital. Rules were laid down and patients only admit-

Founder of Village Hospitals

28. *Dr. Albert Napper, pioneer of village hospitals and founder of Cranleigh Village Hospital c.1860*

ted by the manager in consultation with the Medical Officer on payment of a weekly sum, the amount of which, dependent on family circumstances, was fixed by the Manager. In no sense was it a charitable foundation and, up to the time that it was taken over by the state in 1948, it was entirely self-supporting by admission fees and the very generous support given by the local community, a support which is still much in evidence today. Subscribers had the right to recommend patients for admission to the hospital and Napper insisted from the outset that patients should contribute towards their stay in hospital, although, in cases of extreme poverty this condition was sometimes waived. Originally patients paid 3s. 6d. (18p today) to 10s. (50p), according to circumstances, for which they had full board and lodging as well as medical attention. In the first year 22 patients were admitted, either as accident cases or diseases. The receipts amounted to £190 12s. 0d. and the expenses to £150 10s. 0d.

THE FIRST FOUR YEARS.

The trustees' report in 1863, four years after the hospital opened, show that 100 patients had been admitted during that time, twenty two in the first year for either accidents or disease rising to thirty two in the fourth year. It makes clear that 'many of the cases have been of a severe and dangerous

RULES.

I.

THE Hospital is designed for the accommodation of the Poor when suffering from disease, or from accident; and shall be under the direction of three Trustees, one of whom shall be the Rector of the Parish, who shall also be the acting Manager.

II.

The establishment shall consist of a regular nurse, and another woman for the necessary work of the house. A lady has also kindly promised the benefit of her assistance in all special cases.

III.

The nurse shall at such times as her services are not required in the Hospital, attend poor women at their own homes during their confinements, or other illnesses, on payment of the usual fee.

IV.

Patients shall be received on payment of a weekly sum, the amount of which, dependent on their circumstances, is to be fixed by their employer, in conjunction with the Manager of the Hospital.

V.

Admission of Patients shall be granted by the Manager, on consultation with the Medical Officer, to either of whom applications for admission may be made, addressed, to the Village Hospital, Cranley.

VI.

The Medical Department shall be under the control and superintendence of A. Napper, Esq.

VII.

The Domestic arrangements shall be under the management and supervision of some of the ladies of the parish.

VIII.

Every requisite shall be provided in the Hospital, and patients may not receive food or drink from any other source, without the sanction of the Medical Officer.

IX.

The funds for the establishment and support of the Hospital shall be raised by voluntary contributions, and the Treasurer's statement of the receipts and expenditure (examined by the Trustees), shall be printed once a-year, and forwarded to each subscriber.

X.

All Subscriptions shall be payable yearly and in advance, on the first of October, and any of the Trustees may receive Donations and Subscriptions, an account of which shall be rendered to the Treasurer.

XI.

The furniture, and all other property of the Hospital, shall be vested in the Trustees.

XII.

In case of a vacancy, the remaining Trustees shall elect another to make up the number.

29.
*The
Rules of
the
Village
Hospital
c.1860*

nature: the admission of many railway accidents, which could not have been successfully treated in the huts of the navvies.' The longest stay in hospital was that of a young boy suffering from 'nerosis of the tybia, exision of the diseased bone' who was in hospital for 332 days.

A sample of cases taken from trustees' reports:-

Accidents:

Case 2.   A man. Compound fracture of both bones of the leg
           51 days inpatient

Case 7.   A man. Amputation of the thigh for an injury
           No. days not known

Case 43.   A man. Injury of the eye 71 days inpatient

Case 70.   A man. Dislocation of the ankle with fracture of the tibia and
           fibula 49 days inpatient

Case 82.   A man. Severe scalp wounds 12 days inpatient

Case 93.   A man. Amputation of the arm for an injury also compound
           comminuted fracture of the leg 11 days inpatient

Case 97.   A man. Injury of the knee with severe laceration and haemor-
           rhage 20 days inpatient

Case 99.   A man Laceration of the ligaments of the knee
           9 days inpatient

Diseases of the chest:-

Case 13.   A man. Phthysis pulmonitis 2 days inpatient

Case 11.   A man. Chronic Pneumonia with hydrothorax ascites and
           tympanitis 41 days inpatient

Case 39.   A man. Pneumonia 23 days inpatient

Case 49.   A man. Phthysis 113 days inpatient

Case 55.   A man. Pleurisy 11 days in patient

Case 90.   A man. Pneumonia 28 days in patient

With just a few exceptions the annual reports and accounts showed a credit balance at the end of each year and when the State took over the minute books of the trustees, show that there were sufficient funds in hand to purchase a small annuity for the retiring matron.

Throughout its history there has never been any lack of support for the hospital. The early reports give lists of subscriptions ranging from £5 to 2s.6d with those donating 10s. or more having the right to nominate a sick person for admittance.These sums seem small nowadays but it must be remembered that 2s.6d, the old half crown, was a considerable sum for a farm labourer in the mid 1860s. In 1865 the wages of the nurse and

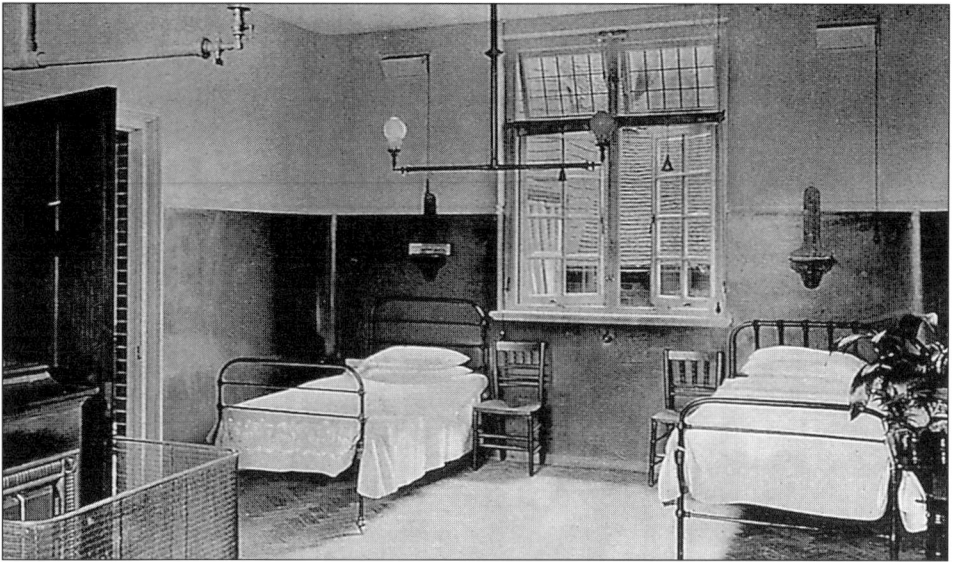

30. *The men's ward in the Cranleigh Village Hospital in the early 1900s*

charwoman totalled £38 per annum whilst firing and lighting cost £9.4s.5d and £11.5s.5d was spent on wine, beer and spirits. Treatment included a liberal diet of meat and wine. The Village Hospital Dietary specifies an ordinary diet consisting of 'Suet and Meat Puddings, and Pies, Meat of all kinds, with vegetables and bread and cheese.' The extra diet allowed in addition, ' extra quantities of Meat for breakfast or supper, Eggs, Poultry, Fish, Jellies, Wine, Brandy, Ale or Porter as specially ordered by the Medical Attendant.' There were four meals a day, breakfast, dinner, tea and supper. It is clear from an article he wrote for the Medical Mirror, that Dr. Napper believed in the efficacy of 'the advantage of good nursing, generous diet and comfortable lodgings' in helping patients' recovery. Cases of Port wine and bottles of spirits were often given to the hospital by the local gentry as well as pheasants, rabbits and other game. As late as 1877 leeches were still in use and in 1868 the following notice appeared in the Annual Report 'Donations of Port Wine and Brandy together with linen rags (for bandages) will be appreciated'. All the early reports give lists of gifts such as rabbits, vegetables, fruit, new laid eggs, linen sheets, flannel jackets - a whole range of items going down to children's toys, scrap books, magazines, and so on.

Dr. Napper who lived in Broad Oak Cottage near the hospital was very definitely 'the Boss' in the hospital and he had his own ideas about nurses as the following quotation from his pamphlet about the hospital demonstrates:

'Most essential in this institution is a good nurse. There can be no question as to the superiority of one well trained and competent in her duties; but on the other hand these advantages are frequently more than counter-balanced by an inordinate amount of conceit, and disinclination to conform to the instructions that do not happen to accord with her preconceived notions; and where the hospital is near the residence of the medical officer, which, in every case, is most desirable, I am not sure that a sensible untutored woman who will strictly carry out the directions given to her will not often be found the more efficacious'.

One suspects that Dr. Napper had had several differences with his nurses and one detects an echo of the obstacles that Florence Nightingale had to face. The hospital was opened just two years after she had returned from the Crimean war, determined to do something about the nursing profession. The author is certain that Dr. Napper must have met and known her.

It is worth noting here that towards the end of the century the Cranleigh and Ewhurst Benefit Nursing Association was formed, and in September 1899 Sir George and Lady Bonham gave a garden party at Knowle Park for members of the association. The report of the occasion in the Surrey Advertiser included the following:

'The Association is at the present time in a most flourishing condition and the recent decision of the committee to engage the services of a third nurse presented itself to Lady Bonham, President of the Association as a fitting occasion to mark its success by some sort of social gathering of the members of the two parishes.' It further notes that: 'Thirty seven cases have been nursed in a period of one hundred and five weeks'.

After Dr. Napper's retirement in 1881 his place was taken by his son Mr. A. A. Napper who had become his father's partner in 1873. He remained as Honorary Medical Officer after his retirement until 1919 when he finally resigned from the governing committee.

Archdeacon Sapte died in 1905 and the Church conveyed the freehold of the cottage to trustees that were appointed from a village meeting to look after the hospital. The first extensions to the original cottage were made between 1901 and 1903 increasing accommodation to eight beds, the costs of the extension being met by voluntary donations. The whole place was completely redecorated in 1909 when the cottage was restored to its original condition, many exposed beams having previously been whitewashed or plastered over. By this time the subscribers began to take an active part in the management of the hospital. In August 1908 the trustees called a general meeting of the village from which a General and Executive Committee was appointed which continued to run the hospital until 1948.

The years of the First World War, 1914-1918, were of course as difficult as for everyone else. In 1915-1916 the 5th battalion of the Oxford and Bucks

Light Infantry were billeted in the village and the Colonel in charge expressed grateful thanks to the staff for the care of his men. It is also recorded that there was a close association between Canadian forces stationed nearby and the hospital.

One of the problems that has always beset the hospital was, and still is, the lack of space in which to expand. The extensions made in the 1920's were made possible by the brewers who owned The Three Horsehoes next door donating a piece of land. A further two pieces of land were bought from Mr. Nightingale and with a generous gift of a portion of Broad Oak garden, room was found for an additional ward of two beds, a room for the matron and other rooms. An appeal to meet the costs of these extensions raised £2,628 and they were opened in 1922, free from debt.

31. *Dr. Albert Arthur Napper, the founder's son and successor at the Village Hospital, probably in the early 1900s*

Still, however, there was a need to extend and in 1936 a firm of London Architects was consulted. They recommended that the existing building be demolished and a new hospital erected on the site. This was reluctantly accepted by a meeting of subscribers by a majority of two, but the outcry in the village was such that an alternative had to be found. The then Parish Clerk who lived in the adjoining house was persuaded to part with a piece of his garden which provided the site for the house which was used for many years as living accommodation for the nurses. This house is now used by the Health Authority for the Mental Health Clinic.

The years of the Second World War were just as difficult, especially with regard to staffing. Twice, the hospital was damaged by blast from air raids but fortunately, no-one was injured. Should the hospital have had to close, it was arranged that everyone would be moved to Baynards. Again, there was a close association with the Armed Forces stationed in the area, especially the Canadians. The Minutes of the Committee record thanks for the gifts of food, medicines and drugs etc., from British Columbia and from Oaklands Red Cross Hospital in Knowle Lane.

When the National Health Service started in 1948 the hospital went fully into the hands of the State. In fact, it had been under state control since the out break of war in 1939 when all such institutions were taken over. It was not long however, before people began to realise that there was still a place for and a need for voluntary help to hospitals, their patients and staff in providing the additional amenities that the basic Health Service was not providing.The League of Friends movement was started in 1949, starting with an appeal for funds to pay for a new treatment room and improved waiting accommodation. £2,058 was raised in four months, an indication of the support that the hospital has always received from the locality. Since then the League has raised and spent many thousands of pounds on improving the facilities of the hospital and providing many things for it. In 1989, when the fortieth anniversary of the movement was celebrated, a garden party was held at Milford Hospital, where it was announced that the five leagues associated with local hospitals, Guildford, Milford, Haslemere, Brookwood and Cranleigh had collectively raised over £2,000,000 for the hospitals and of that sum Cranleigh had contributed over £250,000.

Several times the hospital has been under threat of closure, the most serious occasion being in 1974-5. Fortunately just at that time the adjoining premises, a shop known as the Curio Shop came on the market. After a great deal of pressure from the League and its Chairman, Mr. P. E. Levy, and everyone else in the district, the Authority was persuaded to buy the property but only after the League had agreed to try and raise £25,000 towards the purchase price and the costs of extending the hospital. With the co-operation of everyone in Cranleigh, Ewhurst and the surrounding areas that sum of money was raised in 17 weeks. The Authority took its time to develop the site and the enlarged hospital was not opened until 1981 by which time the appeal fund had grown with donations from all quarters and accumulated interest to over £90,000 which enabled the building of the consulting room, the equipping of the physiotheraphy clinic and also to pay for the garden for the disabled, designed and developed by the students of the Merrist Wood Agricultural College.

The mention of such sums of money prompts a return for the moment to the reports of earlier days. It is interesting to recall what was paid in wages to the staff. For example, in 1906 one, Elizabeth Taylor, was engaged as a servant at £18 per year, the lighting of the heating apparatus being one of her duties. Even in 1937 the nurse's annual salary was only £65 per year and was then raised to £70. The scale of charges to be paid by patients was increased in 1911 to 3 shillings(15p) a week for children under 14, labourers and their families from 3-5 shillings whilst private patients paid two guineas. In 1907 and in the following years a 'Pound Day' was held in Cranleigh when everyone who could gave a pound of something to the hospital.

We take pride in Cranleigh in the fact that this was the first Cottage Hospital in the country. Of course there were hospitals in large towns. In the Middle Ages monasteries played their part and from the reign of the first Elizabeth there were the Poor Law institutions and infirmaries run by local Boards of Guardians but Cranleigh Village Hospital, run and supported entirely by minimal charges and voluntary contributions from local people, was unique in its time. It is small now by modern standards with only 14 beds, mainly for post operative, geriatric and terminal cases and to some it may seem hardly worth keeping open, yet the running costs compare very favourably with the larger hospitals. With the adjacent health centre it has now become a valuable and viable part of the health services for the district. There is close co-operation between hospital and health centre, the doctors in the practice regularly attending patients in the hospital. One of the most gratifying results of the enlargement of the hospital in 1981 was that rooms were provided in the extended building so that consultants could come from Guildford to hold clinics and thus obviate journeys to Guildford for attention.

A postscript ends the story. If you go into the churchyard of St. Nicolas church, there you will find the grave of John Henry Sapte, Archdeacon and rector of Cranleigh and a few steps away the family tomb of the Nappers.There they lie, clergyman and doctor, just across the road from the work they started 140 years ago.

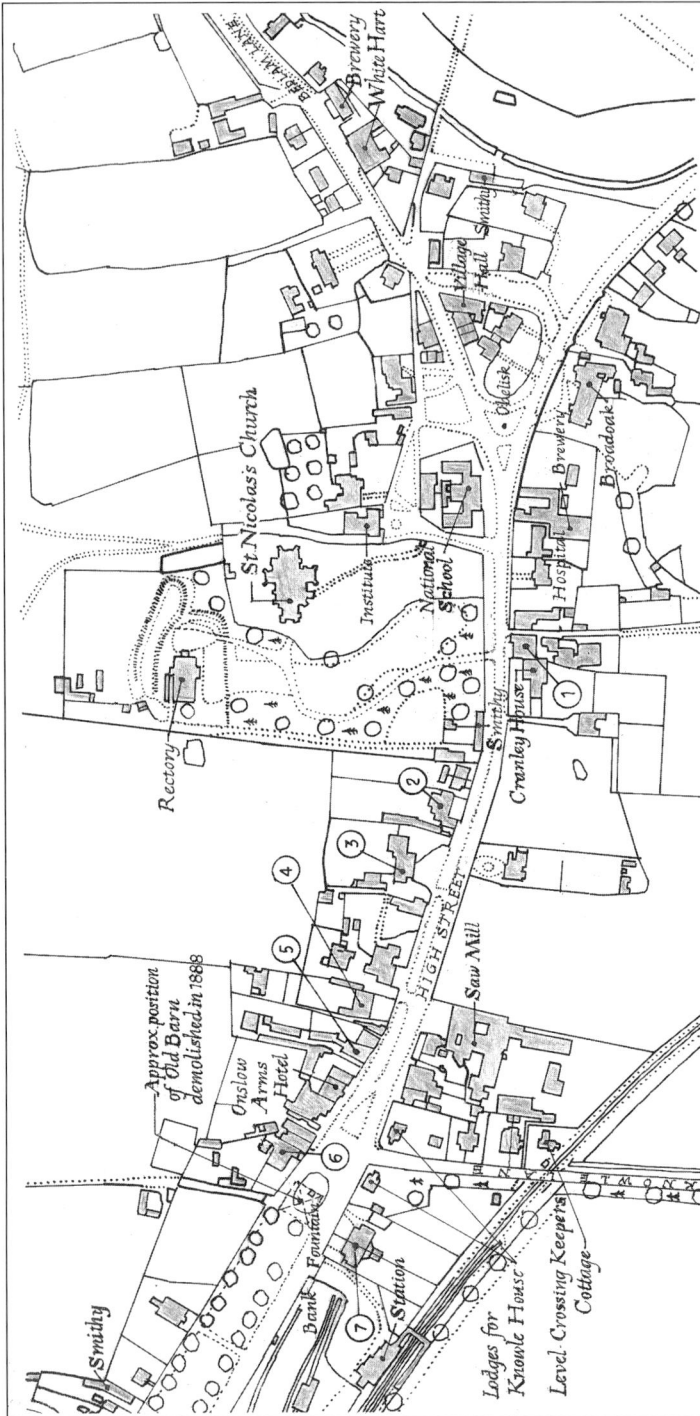

Cranleigh 1891

800 Feet

St Nicolas's Church

Rectory

Institute

National School

Smithy

Cranley House

Obelisk

Village Hall

Smithy

Brewery

White Hart

Hospital

Brewery

Broadoak

Saw Mill

HIGH STREET

Approx position of Old Barn demolished in 1888

Onslow Arms Hotel

Smithy

Bank

Fountain

Station

Lodges for Knowle House

Level Crossing Keeper's Cottage

① Freeland House – now 'Nizam Indian Restaurant'.

② Collins Stores – now 'Brown's Estate Agents' and 'Baby Shop'.

③ 'The Greyhound' Public House – now the Post Office.

④ 'Oliver House – now 'Cromwell Tea Rooms' and Bradley's Florist'.

⑤ Mann's & Co. Ltd – now 'Manns of Cranleigh'.

⑥ Ivy Hall Farm – now 'La Chacouterie', 'Attwell & Rogers', and 'Wine Rack.'

⑦ Grahams – originally two private houses: later, one private house and one lodging house.

Based upon the Ordnance Survey Map of 1891

84

CHAPTER 6

SHOPPING IN CRANLEIGH 1850 - 1990

It is said that one of the most popular leisure activities of the nineteen nineties is shopping, or rather window shopping. A day can be spent wandering through large, bright Malls or department stores, tempted by luxury items and strengthened by coffee or burgers. What would our great, or great, great, grandmothers have thought of this?

In the mid nineteenth century the population of Cranley consisted almost entirely of agricultural workers and until the railway made the area easily accessible the population remained fairly stable at around 1,300. Many labourers lived on their farms while others rented small cottages. The domestic round was simple but hard. Very little meat other than home-grown pork was eaten and fruit and vegetables came from your own plot. Bread was home-baked in wood-fired ovens because coal, brought along the canal to Elmbridge Wharf, cost 30s a ton and was a luxury bought by the rich. Coming into Cranley to buy your essentials was probably a social event, gossip was exchanged and family events discussed. What would those inhabitants have found when they arrived along the muddy road, past the windmill grinding corn and the barn and pond of Ivy Hall Farm? Most of the shops were situated along the north of The Street as it was then called. Along the south side of the road ran a drainage ditch and every property was reached via a bridge.

William Welch described a walk along Cranley Street in 1846 [1]. After Ivy Hall Farm, now Attwell and Rogers, Wine Rack and the Delicatessen, there were three shops whose owners sound like Happy Families: Mr. Snatt the harnessmaker, Mr. Hedger the tailor and Mr. Stedman the shoemaker. Immediately we see the difference in the needs of village shoppers. Harnesses, not for leisure use, but because horses provided the principal means of transport, tailor because 'ready to wear' did not exist and clothes were home-made or tailored to order and shoemaker with no fancy shelves of shoes to choose from, just a good, strong pair of boots to be made.

After the Onslow Arms another shoemaker, Mr. Killick. These premises were usually workshops and living quarters, not the showroom type of shop we see today. Next we find the grocer and baker Mr. Warner. What would he have sold? All the ingredients needed for good, plain home cooking, flour, sugar, tea, butter, cheese, dried fruit, spices, and so on, all weighed loose and put in paper bags. Beyond stood a house later to become the Greyhound Inn [now the Post Office] but still a private residence at this time, then another grocer, Gumbrells using premises next to the old house known as Spittledyke Cottage, now Browns, Estate Agents. This had for many years been the home of a family called Lee, who were weavers. Next to this was one of many smiths, Laker's Smithy. Behind the new school we find Mr. Puttock the wheelwright and Mr. Farmer the butcher as well as the Malthouse.

On the south side of the street stood the home of the Rowland family, Freeland House, now the Indian Restaurant Nizam. This has been a shop since 1603 and at this time was a drapers. Next door, across South Street, Mr. Crewdson kept his cabinet maker's shop. He was also the post master and renowned for the interest he took in other people's mail. Further along, opposite the Onslow Arms, Mrs. Harington dispensed 'medicines', including Holloway's pills, and Mr. Holden had his plumbing and timber business.

Sunday trading does not seem to be a new idea. It was necessary for the Rector, the newly appointed Rev. Sapte, to write to the 'shopkeepers of Cranley Parish' to refrain from selling goods on Sundays. The letter of agreement was signed by Henry Gumbrell, Henry Rowland and James Warner among others. Charles Harington, the chemist, agreed not to sell anything except medicine and leeches. It is interesting to see that two shopkeepers, Joshua Ingold and Thomas Stemp were unable to write their names and 'made their mark'.

By the turn of the century much had changed in Cranleigh, as we were now to be called to avoid the post office confusing us with Crawley. The Street became grandly called the High Street and the drainage ditch was filled in. People came to live here who worked up or down the railway line and the village was 'filled in' between the Ewhurst and Horsham roads by the entrepreneurial Mr.Rowland causing the population to rise to over 2,000 and by 1901 to over 2,700. How did this change the shops? It seems very little. More people needed more goods and many of these 'incomers' were wealthier than the original inhabitants but there had not been a sufficient change in the way of life to change the type of shops. Food was mainly locally produced and seasonal - no strawberries in January! - and clothes were home or tailor-made. Local transport was still by cart, carriage or on foot so the number of shops increased but not their variety.

Looking at the High Street in the 1890s we find the shops still cater for the demands of a relatively self-sufficient community. On entering the High Street from the Common there is still a smith, James Peters and a harness maker, John Snatt. Ivy Hall Farm has lost its pond and barn but is still a home now housing the post office. Beyond the farm we find a watchmaker. Has the arrival of the railway made the local inhabitants more time conscious? A shoemaker, Mr. Puttock and saddler James Ruddle come next, then Mr. Farmer the butcher can still be patronised. After the Onslow Arms a small furniture store - to furnish all the new properties being built - was thriving, soon to enlarge to become the still popular David Mann's. Before the Greyhound, now an inn, the Winser family is running a grocery business and coal merchants. Mr. Randall, the shoe and bootmaker, lives and

33. *John Randall, shoemaker, poses outside his workshop-home with his wife, child, and probably an apprentice*

works in a house later to become Barclay's Bank. After the inn was another grocery and drapers run by the Gumbrells but soon to be Collins and then the smith, George Laker.

Behind the new school there can be found Cheesman's wheelwrights shop. Opposite, Rowlands' drapery and grocery business in Freeland House was followed by a new draper and supplier of 'clothing and boots', Tanner and Chart. In London House, demolished in the 1960's to make way for a new set of shops - Midland Bank, Unwins and Mann's Estate Agents - Walter Briggs sold linen, clothes and boots. This later became another draper and ladies' dress shop called Gammons. We have a new chemist, Mr. George Vennell, and the Holden family, (George and Son were builders and timber merchants and David a plumber and decorator) seem to have the Cranleigh building scene 'all tied up'.

Cranleigh 1913

800 FEET

0

① Freeland House – now 'Nizam Indian Restaurant'.
② Collins Stores – now 'Brown's Estate Agents' and 'Baby Shop'.
③ 'The Greyhound' Public House – now the Post Office.
④ 'Oliver House – now 'Cromwell Tea Rooms' and Bradley's Florist'.
⑤ Mann's & Co. Ltd – now 'Manns of Cranleigh'.
⑥ Ivy Hall Farm – now 'La Chacouterie', 'Attwell & Rogers', and 'Wine Rack'.
⑦ Grahams – originally two private houses: later, one private house and one lodging house.

Based upon the Ordnance Survey Map of 1913

88

35. *Cheesman's wheelwright's workshop opposite the obelisk, pictured c.1902*

ROAD TRANSPORT ARRIVES TO BRING CHANGES

As with the arrival of the railway, the major changes in the first part of the new century came because of transport, this time on the road. A few people had their own cars and the more successful shops obtained delivery vans. A bus service ran to Guildford, a very uncomfortable journey so it was said. Very popular for men and women as well as delivery boys was the bicycle. Looking at the new shops in Cranleigh we see a reflection of this change, as car and cycle mechanics and garages appear. The first Osbourn's, grandly known as the National Motor, Cycle and General Engineers, was opened in the Ewhurst Road, later to move to the site of the present Little Manor Garage. This had been our local brewery, Bruford's. Whittington's cycle shop was also to be found in the Ewhurst Road and yet another cycle shop came just before the obelisk. In the High Street we have the Onslow Motor Co. and after Knowle Lane another cycle shop, Mr. Quick's. Beyond the Methodist Church, Mr. Kelf's shop sold cycle accessories. David Mann's made their own bicycle known as 'The Enterprise'.

There was new development opposite the station by now, including a terrace of shops known as Bank Buildings due to the position of Capital and Counties Bank on the corner of Rowland Road. James Carpenter ran a bakery and Mr. Delves owned a double shop, running one as a hairdressers, advertising 'all kinds of ornamental hair work', the other was run as a stationer's and tobacconist. The Gas and Water Offices came next then Donkins the greengrocer. Across Rowland Road, Weller's, the auctioneers

36. *One of the buildings in Bank Buildings in 1910 was Mr. Carpenter's Bakery, with tea rooms.*

Telephone 102.   Established 1910.

C. G. CRICK & SON

Northampton Boot Stores
(2 doors from the Wesleyan Church),

CRANLEIGH.

The well-known House for

BOOTS
and
SHOES

and all Accessories.

Agencies : " LOTUS," " DELTA," " ORAL,"
CLARK'S " TOR," etc.

REPAIRS OF EVERY DESCRIPTION DONE ON
THE PREMISES.

52

had an office until it was pulled down to build another bank, The London and Counties Bank, which became the Westminster Bank. After Mr. Parsons the saddler, still in business despite the modern trend for motorised transport, was Ivy Hall Farmhouse, now entirely a shop, Tyler's the grocer, a landmark in Cranleigh for many years. Crick's shoe shop came next until it moved to a shop beyond the Methodist Church and after a toy shop came the fish shop. David Mann had enlarged to its present frontage now incorporating Cromwell Cottage as a furniture showroom. Winsers, in Kent House, sold a variety of merchandise: it was a bakery, grocery, tea shop and coal dealers. Beyond the Greyhound Inn, Collins' grocery and famous pork butchers was gaining in popularity. Opposite, on what is now the most recent hospital extension, stood Nightingale's china and furniture shop, also selling brooms and lamp oil which shows modern living had not come to all. Several new shops were built along the south side of the High Street which had been largely residential; a saddler's, newsagents, the Onslow Motor Co. and new premises for Cheesmans' wheelwrights' business.

An exciting arrival was the cinema, in a corrugated iron building behind Mr. Lanchberry's tobacconist

38. *The staff of Collins shop – Family Grocer and Provision Merchant as well as Pork Butcher – stand proudly outside their shop in 1912. The two men in suits are Robert and George Collins.* By kind permission of R. Collins

shop. It is believed that his wife played the piano in this time of silent films. This original cinema building survived until very recently being used as a warehouse by the old Co-op food store. It was demolished in 1998. Next a large drapery and clothes shop now Gammons, supplied the ladies of the village with their commodious underwear, hosiery and dresses, skirts and hats. After the watchmaker and a sweet shop the lodge house for Knowle House stood on the corner, its partner opposite having been demolished to build the post office [now Holman's jewellers]. Attwell's chemist shop, still a chemist today, sold a delightful remedy called 'Kurakoff' at only 1s 3d a bottle.

Latest Styles in
MILLINERY.
FANCY ,
DRAPERY.
BABY LINEN.

— ø —

A Large Assortment of

BLOUSES,
JUMPERS,
SPORTS
COATS, etc.

— ø —

Wedding and ,
Mourning Orders
executed at the
Shortest Notice.

— ø —

Always replete with
Latest Novelties.

MISS ELLIOTT,
Gainsborough House, CRANLEIGH.

The houses later to become Grahams were still a private dwelling, part of which was a lodging house where many of the bank clerks stayed.

The station buildings were set back from the road with a coal storage area to one side. The coal merchant occupied the 'Old Bank', a building used for this purpose before the more modern branches over the road were built. Another small building housed W. H. Smith who provided papers and magazines for the commuters using the station. Beyond the station several new shops were built to serve the increasing population. A milliner was very necessary in the days when no lady would be seen without a hat. Then came a very interesting cycle shop owner who also advertised himself as a ventriloquist available for parties. Next, more food shops, including a branch of the chain of International Stores, and smaller shops who all 'waited upon families daily'. On the corner of St. James' Place stood another large drapery and clothes shop, Rowells, who sold calico, flannelette, sheetings, hosiery, gloves and fancy goods as well as ladies' and gents' outfits and overcoats.

TWO LOCAL RESIDENTS REMEMBER THEIR SCHOOLDAYS

Coming into the 1930 to 1940 period we have some present residents who remember the High Street. Two schoolboys, Charlie Croxford and Roy Foster who walked every day from the common to the school recollect a busy and thriving shopping centre.

In the early thirties there was still no cinema opposite the pond but a cobblers and some open ground used as allotments. A newsagent stood on the site of Cranleigh News but instead of placing a bet you might have bought shoes or boots from the corner shop. Across St. James' Place, Rowell and Hill still flourished as ladies' and gentleman's outfitters. Although there were still some residential properties along this side of the common there was also a selection of shops selling, not the specialised goods of a marginal shopping area, as we have today, but the necessities of ordinary living. There were two butchers and a greengrocer/fish shop, the International Stores and Crick's grocery all doing good business, as well as cleaners, milliners, clockmaker, wool shop, cycle and ironmongers and a stationer and tobacconist. This was obviously an area used daily for ordinary, domestic shopping. Beyond the Methodist Church was Wellers the corn chandler and then the station with its front yard full of coal. Corndale, the boarding house [now Grahams] stood next to Attwells the chemist where the front room of the living accommodation had been turned into an optician's shop after the qualification of Hillman Attwell's son. Another new arrival to sell and service 'modern' equipment was Farrows Wireless and Electrical shop before the Post Office and Telephone Exchange on the corner of Knowle Lane. The Co-op, on the other corner, originally selling groceries and meat was followed by another sweet shop, Loves, then

---

The Cheapest and Best Watch on the Market—**RAVENHILL'S 18.6,** Jewelled movement, warranted 2 yrs.

The Clock .

House, . .

Cranleigh, .

THE PLACE FOR **REPAIRS** to WATCHES, CLOCKS, JEWELLERY, and PLATED GOODS.

A Good Assortment of **GOLD, SILVER & FANCY GOODS** always in Stock.

Best Workmanship.

MODERATE PRICES.

20 Years' Clerkenwell Experience.

ALL REPAIRS executed within seven days.

Lucas's Cranleigh Pictorial Guide and Directory.

CHARLES RAVENHILL, "THE CLOCK HOUSE," CRANLEIGH.

'Clockhouse' run by Ravenhills, and then Howards. By the late thirties the house and shop run by Mr. Lanchberry had been demolished to make room for the new Co-op, now demolished in its turn, and the cinema in the corrugated shed became their warehouse when the smart new cinema opened.

Warrens' builders yard, previously Holdens, left a gap in the buildings to be followed by the fishmonger and butchers still on the same sites today. Some undeveloped plots still existed and one of these was a house called 'The Elms', the home of Dr. Cameron. Another was used to build the second chemist for the village, Dan Clare who sold 'English and Foreign Patent Medicines'. The Village Hall was opened in 1933. Beyond it there was at this time and for many years to come a newsagent and tobacconist owned by Napletons. The last owners of the business, Ron and Marion Haley, sold out in 1990 when it became yet another estate agents, and then came an ironmongers, the forerunner of the DIY shop of today. The attractive black and white building next was the Sundial Cafe run by Mrs. Smallridge. Cranleigh House Hotel, on the Library site was followed by Freeland House, a sweet and grocery shop, and Nightingales' furniture and cycle shop next to the Three Horseshoes Public House. The old brewery, now defunct, was Osbourns' Garage soon to become Cranleigh Motors.

The shops along the Ewhurst Road, like those facing the common, were far more utilitarian than today. They included a photographer, toy shop, grocers and greengrocers, a dairy, sweet and wool shops, a butcher and a cobbler (moved from his original shop by the building of the cinema).

Back in the High Street Collins Pork Butchers was thriving but The Greyhound next door had unfortunately closed down. Barclays Bank was built on the site of the garden of Kent House which was still a grocery business. A new bakery - to become Hibbs - was opened by Mr. Cornwall, the last publican of The Greyhound. In Oliver House a visiting dentist, Mr. Peetling, held his surgery in the part of the house he shared with a gentleman's tailor and, at one time a small school attended by both Mr. and Mrs. Roy Collins. The remainder of the house was still a private residence occupied by Jesse Mann who ran the large shop next door.

Part of the Onslow Arms, now the Bradford and Bingley, was the Pals' Club Room. This ex - Servicemen's club not only formed a social function but was a kind of Friendly Society helping to pay sickness benefit and funeral expenses. The three lovely old shops beyond were now Mrs. Hales' fish shop, the Oak Room Cafe and bakery and the bookshop. After Tylers, an estate agent and the Westminster bank we cross Rowland Road. Bank Buildings was still a busy shopping area - another bank and Estate Agent a foretaste of things to come, then Mr. Donkins the greengrocer, the Singing Kettle Cafe, the showrooms of the Guildford Gas, Light and Coke Company who offered the 'two finest servants every household needed'. Stopping whilst shopping for a cup of tea and a bun was obviously a common event judging by the number of cafes. Perhaps the walk to the village and the thought of carrying the shopping home encouraged the appetite.

During these inter-war years Cranleigh was a mainly agricultural community going about its own business. Shopping, apart from an outing to Guildford or Horsham for important items, was local. Anything heavy was willingly - and freely - delivered. Mainly non-working wives still shopped daily making the village shops not only a source of the necessities of life but a valuable social network

MEMORIES OF A CRANLEIGH CHILD

Brenda Goodchild was born and brought up on Smithwood Common and can remember the village shops she passed on her way to school every day: 'In the 1930s and 1940s there were a lot more shops in the village than we have now, and it was a much nicer place to live. Everyone knew nearly all the people as it was so much less populated, and we had so many more shops for choice, and if you couldn't get to the village, living like I did at Smithwood Common, and not any buses, most of the people would come to your door. There was the oil man called Mr. Kelf, who had a van, and came round once a week and brought oil for your lamps and stoves, and Sunlight soap for your washing, candles, soda, matches, blue bag, to make your sheets white. And then the baker would call every other day with bread, cakes and flour. The milkman didn't call in the early 30's so we got our milk from a farm, taking a can every day. My father grew all our own vegetables, early potatoes, then the main crop, cabbage, spring greens, purple sprouting, brussels sprouts, parsnips, marrows, carrots, broad beans, runner beans, peas, beetroot and onions. The beetroot you pickled for the winter, as well as onions, you made marrow chutney and rhubarb jam, plum jam, apple and blackberry jam. My father got all his seeds from the Corn Stores in the village, which is now a restaurant. It has been many different restaurants since it was a Corn Stores. Then it was a big store which had a different smell when you went in it, all hay and oats and an earthy smell of potatoes, in sacks and onions. You could buy all your seeds there, seed potatoes, runner beans, peas were all sold loose, you bought a gill or half a gill, you got hay and oats for your horse, corn for your chickens. I think flower seeds were in packets. They had forks, spades, everything for your garden and your animals and in wartime, which I remember most, everyone had an allotment as well as digging up your own garden so you needed a lot of seeds.

When my mother did go shopping we had a great choice, there were three quite big grocers' stores, the Co-op, International Stores and Forest Stores. In the Co-op where nearly everything was sold loose, no packets of biscuits, they were in big square tins with clear lids, tipped up a bit so you could see them, then the assistant would weigh out half a pound or one pound, all put in blue bags, the same with sugar and tea. At the Co-op you even got bread tokens and milk tokens for the week and put them out for the baker and milkman. On the bacon counter the assistants wore big white aprons and cut the bacon while you waited, how you wanted it, it tasted like bacon, not all sealed up in plastic. The butter was off a big block and using two butter pats, was patted into shape on the greaseproof paper and then into blue bags, the same with lard and cheese. If you couldn't get to the shops the Co-op and the other shops had a delivery service which you had two books, one you gave to the man with your order and when he bought it, you paid and gave him the other book with your next week's order, if you forgot something you went without until next week.

We had two fish shops, four butchers, as well as Rowell and Hills, drapers and Co-op drapers, we had Gammons too; all sold shoes, clothes for ladies and children and a men's department, underwear, linen, blankets, curtains. In Gammons you had a Lamson Tube, which was a tube system that went round the shop above your head to the cashier and if your goods came to eleven pence three farthings instead of giving you a farthing change you would get a packet of pins. As well as the three drapers' shops selling shoes, you had two more shoe shops. There were five paper shops that sold tobacco, cigarettes and sweets and lots of sweet shops, three greengrocers as well as selling fruit and vegetables, you could get a pennyworth of speckled fruit and there was always a whiff of vinegar as it was sold in a big barrel and you bought your own bottle for half a pint or a pint.

There were two hardware shops, Nightingales and Manns. They sold everything you can think of. Paraffin was sold by the canful, you brought your own can and had what you wanted everything was sold loose, you could have 1 lb of nails or two nails, screws bolts, gas mantles, brushes, brooms, paint, soap. In the back room was second-hand furniture and upstairs new furniture, chairs tables, sideboards, rugs, linoleum, carpets, china and glass. There were two barbers, two coal merchants, two clock repairers, a tobacconist which only sold tobacco for your pipe as most men smoked in those days, I think due to being in the First World War.

We had a shop called The Dairy which sold fresh milk and made their own butter and cream. Two or three bakers which baked their own bread, cakes and pastries who all delivered. Three or four tea rooms, two dry cleaners, two flower shops, two stationers which sold writing paper, pens, pencils, books, toys and games and Percy Elliott even had a lending library and Cranleigh Crest china.

Every tradesman played his part in village life, the carpenter, the black-smith, the cobbler, the miller and tailor.'

The author of this section, Anne Woodford, also remembers: 'I moved to Cranleigh in 1961 and was delighted to have my groceries delivered by Tylers and my greengrocery by Mr. Martin in the Fruit Shop. A baker called regularly as well as a supplier of farm eggs. One needed to go out most days for fresh meat and fish and this was a pleasantly social part of the day. It was still unusual to travel far for shopping - indeed on hearing I was about to catch the train for London for the day the cobbler, Mr.Crick commented, 'Why do you want to go there? I haven't been to Guildford for thirty years!' There was still a good variety of shops in the Ewhurst Road, including Westcott Dairy, a grocer and greengrocer, cycle shop, electrician and radio shop, toy shop and cobbler. One of the most fascinating shops in Cranleigh, then situated next to the cobbler was Musicraft. This sold an amazing selection of china and glass ornaments as well as records - a real Aladdin's cave. Food shops, always the basis of a thriving village, were changing with the times as well. Even the smaller ones offered some kind of self-service and freezers appeared, full of ready-made meals, out of season vegetables and ice cream. Very little was now sold loose. My children never had the thrill of a few pence worth of broken biscuits! It was still possible though to choose your desired thickness of bacon in Tylers.'

CRANLEIGH EXPANDS INTO THE SIXTIES

In the mid nineteen sixties Cranleigh grew rapidly. The Glebelands Estate was already established and the building of hundreds of houses on new estates to the east and south of the village increased the population to over 10,000 in 1971.

Opposite the common there was Cricketfield Stores and farther along the International Stores but most of the other food shops in this area had moved or closed. Perhaps because there was little development on the west side of the village it 'died' first.

When the railway closed in 1965 the station buildings were very quickly pulled down and a new shopping precinct known as Stocklund Square was built bringing us our first supermarket, Keymarkets. The other new shops included another chemist, the toy shop (removed from Ewhurst Road), a laundrette, furniture and china shop, a travel agent, shoe shop, supplier of smoked salmon and a shop for decorating materials. The Westminster Bank, now the Natwest Bank also took up residence at one end of the square leaving its old premises to become Cosco, an electrical and television dealers which had previously been in Freeland House.

Was Cranleigh still the centre for most people's shopping? For food and everyday needs it seems so but for more expensive items such as furniture and clothing the choice in the Guildford shops for the ever more mobile shopper was beginning to tell. Compared with the early years of the century we find the large shops, such as ladies' and gentlemen's outfitters, as they referred to themselves, disappearing. Gammons and Rowells closed and the Co-op only held on for a few more years. Smaller specialist shops such as John Graham, previously Jack and Jill, and John Alan survived. Nightingales' furniture shop closed to be demolished eventually for the new hospital extension.

We see fewer teashops and cafes but an increase in places to eat out in the evening. We can choose to have Chinese, Indian or Italian dinners and even

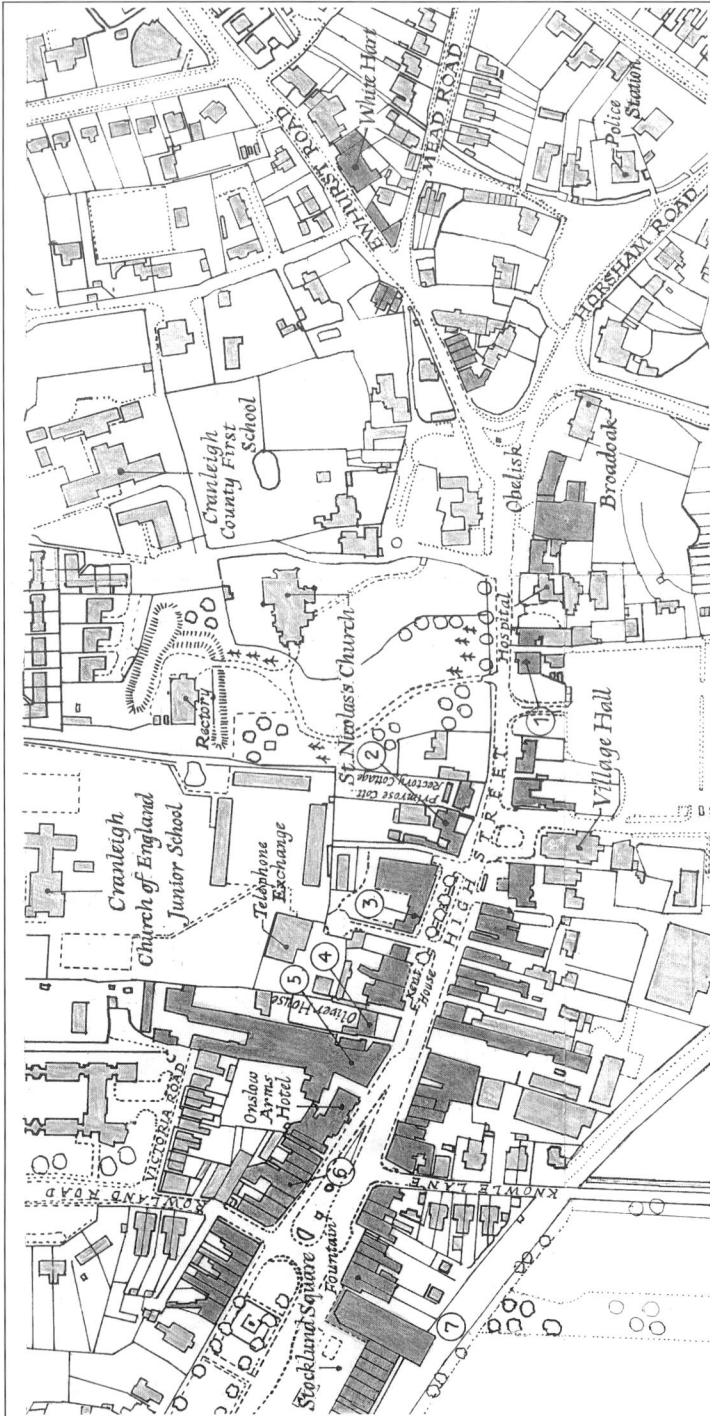

Cranleigh 1970

0   800 FEET

ENHURST ROAD

MEAD ROAD

White Hart

HORSHAM ROAD

Police Station

Cranleigh County First School

Obelisk

Broadoak

Hospital

St Nicolas's Church

Rectory

HIGH STREET

Village Hall

Cranleigh Church of England Junior School

Telephone Exchange

PRIMROSE COTT

RECTORY COTTAGE

② ①

③

④ ⑤

VICTORIA ROAD

Oliver House

Knoll House

Onslow Arms Hotel

ROWLAND ROAD

Stockland Square

Fountain

⑥

KNOWLE LANE

⑦

① Freeland House – now 'Nizam Indian Restaurant'.
② Collins Stores – now 'Brown's Estate Agents' and 'Baby Shop'.
③ 'The Greyhound' Public House – now the Post Office.
④ Oliver House – now 'Cromwell Tea Rooms' and Bradley's Florist'.
⑤ Mann's & Co. Ltd – now 'Manns of Cranleigh'.
⑥ Ivy Hall Farm – now 'La Chacouterie', 'Atwell & Rogers', and 'Wine Rack.'
⑦ Grahams – originally two private houses: later, one private house and one lodging house.

Based upon the Ordnance Survey Map of 1970

98

the pubs began to serve evening meals, as likely to be lasagne or curry as 'bangers and mash!' Take-aways became increasingly cosmopolitan with Chinese and Indian vying with our own fish and chips.

With the increase in home ownership the relevant service industries moved in. It seemed that Estate Agents and Building Societies multiplied overnight at one time. As the population of Cranleigh enlarged they dealt with not only new residents but the increasing habit of moving within the village.

These post 1960 changes marked the way for years to come.The opening of two and eventually three supermarkets must have affected the sales of meat and vegetables from the specialist shops. It is easier to pick up every-thing one needs in one trolley after a day's work after all, but we still have two excellent butchers who have had to develop more exotic lines, a fresh fish shop and a greengrocer. The Delicatessen tempts us with food we only saw on a trip to France a few years ago. The current interest in health and organic food is also catered for while the modern trend to drink wine at home has led to the opening of three off-licences.

With clothes we have been faithful to the well known and tried shops. John Graham, John Alan and until recently, Asparagus for ladies, continue to attract a local clientele but the many smaller boutique-type shops which have opened have had a short life. Shoes are still available, a great boon for mothers who do not wish to drag unwilling young feet round Guildford, and we still have a bookshop, a great advantage in a village but, as yet, no access to a wide selection of music on tape or compact disc.

Our health is catered for by three chemists, and three keep-fit centres. Instead of exercising ourselves by walking to the village we now drive there and pay to use machines to develop our muscles!

Shops that would have amazed our grandparents have also arrived: home security [not long ago you didn't bother to lock your door all day]; and car radios, mobile phones, computer retailers and photocopying facilities. A popular new arrival is the weekly market held in the Village Hall Car Park. This makes Thursday morning now the busiest day of the week with extra business for the permanent shops as well.

Cranleigh is no longer the quiet, rural backwater of the last century. Traffic chokes the High Street and houses have spread over the green fields. A far more affluent population now calls the village home and thinks nothing of driving ten miles on a shopping expedition. Working women are too busy to wander from shop to shop and many residents commute to work, leav-ing early in the morning and returning late in the evening.

Compared with some shopping centres we are lucky that the out-of-town supermarkets have not killed our local shops. These have survived by understanding their market and providing for a more specialised demand than their predecessors. Mr. Godfrey Matthews of John Alan said he was succeeding because he did not bulk buy but carefully selected just what he knew his customers wanted. There are certainly fewer grocers and general stores but to fill these gaps have come the shops catering for the modern demands - computers instead of cobblers, mobile phones instead of milliners.

Cranleigh has grown and changed beyond the imaginings of the shoppers of 1850. The personal and friendly atmosphere still exists though, whether one is buying a crusty loaf, a pound of sausages or meeting friends for morning coffee. Frank Swinnerton, a long time resident, summed up the situation when he said Cranleigh 'grows and as it grows it takes in its new population....without ceasing to be its old good humoured self'.

CHAPTER 7

CONCLUSION

We began this project with the idea of studying continuity and change in the community, two seemingly irreconcilable aspects of all our lives. Even those readers young enough to have been born in the age of space travel, computers and supermarkets are conscious of great changes. Mobile phones, shopping via the internet, and scares about genetically modified foodstuffs have all arrived within the last few years.

The philantrophists of a more than a century ago, who provided the school and the hospital, have been succeeded by the National Health Service and the Education Department. In 1800, there was no hospital at all. Now we have the original hospital, still in use, supported, in part as originally by fundraising from the community through the efforts of its League of Friends. It has been joined by a health centre, dentists, opticians, and a range of other health services all reflecting the same professional concern for patient health that inspired their predecessors. The dame schools of the early 1800s have given way to nursery, primary and secondary education within the village; slates and multiplication tables have given way to computers; further and higher education and life long learning is available to all.

Changes in communications range from penny post to e-mail, from turnpike roads to space travel, yet there is still a need for goods to be carried from place to place, to satisfy customers' needs, just as Knight, Elliot and Beadell did in the last century. There is still a role here in supplying the daily needs of the village and in promoting trade. Cranleigh may not be a major town, but it has a weekly market, and a very real role in supplying its hinterland with a wide range of services which have developed as part of the community's growth over two centuries. It was once a largely self-sufficient village with individual traders supplying largely homemade goods relevant to local needs. Now, in a day and age of large out of town supermarkets, it still has a wide range of individual shops and the range of goods and services available still serve daily needs, often in the same buildings that have provided the same goods and services for many years. What changes in the community's needs do they reflect? What has been lost, and what gained? What might be the community's future needs?

What then of continuity? Living in a village whose beginnings are lost in unrecorded time, all changes seem to come as part of strands of living history. Yes, we are dismayed by traffic, but was not the first motor car in Cranleigh seen by some as the end of life as they knew it? The education and health of our children is still foremost in our thoughts, whether a modern school and health centre cater for them or a 'wise woman' and an apprenticeship with the local smith. Continuity comes often through families. We now have many more families, smaller in size than two hundred years ago, lower child mortality and more working mothers, yet there are still Cranleigh residents whose names appear on the oldest records of births, marriages and deaths we can find.

Continuity also comes from a desire for a community, that very subtle characteristic that makes it a good place to live. There are many aspects of Cranleigh's past not covered in this, or indeed any other book available. Now, all events are recorded so thoroughly by the media that we can feel we are living them again. We all stepped on to the moon with Armstrong. How marvellous to have landed in the New World with Columbus! The past two hundred years are documented fairly well and records are available, but the curious historian is still left with tantalising gaps into the thoughts and events that fashioned the lives of the man in the street. This was the impetus of our investigations and we hope it has not only interested you but made you wonder about the past of your own family and community.

43. Car in the Horsham Road, at the end of 1999

REFERENCES

Abbreviations: SHC – Surrey History Centre   St. N. – St. Nicolas School, Cranleigh.

Chapter 2: Communications
1. Christopher Budgen, Cranleigh: A History of Wealden Settlement (Wealden Publishing, 1998)
2. Hilaire Belloc, The Stane Street (Constable, 1913)
3. W. T. R. Pryce (ed), Studying Family and Community History: 19th and 20th Centuries. Vol. 2 . From Family History to Community History, Series editor: Ruth Finnegan. (C.U.P. in association with the Open University 1994)
4. Kelly's Directories for Surrey, 1852 & 1903
5. A History of the Village, Shamley Green History Society, 1993
6. Dorian Gerhold, Road Transport Before the Railways (C. U. P., 1993)
7. Act of Parliament: 58 Geo III , c.69
8. Christopher Budgen, Cranleigh: A History of Wealden Settlement (Wealden Publishing, 1998)
9. Michael Miller, Around Cranleigh (Chalford,1996)
10. H. E. Malden, (ed), The Victoria History of the Counties of England, Parts 12 & 14 (Constable 1912)
11. Samuel Mann, Cranleigh in Ye Olden Days & Cranleigh Today (1930. Southern Reprographics. Reprinted and updated 1985)
12. *Ibid.*
13. Rev. Owen Manning and William Bray, The History and Antiquities of the County of Surrey, (E. P. Publishing Ltd in collaboration with Surrey County Library. Reprinted 1974)
14. A. Everitt, Country, County and Town, (Transactions of the RHS,1979)
15. Stephen Hampton, Country Carriers of West Surrey: A Study of the Guildford Area 1850 - 1950 (Unpublished thesis submitted for M.A. degree in English Local History, Leicester University, 1971)
16. Lasham's Guildford Almanac and Directory, 1851, 1859, 1882, 1903, 1912
17. Stephen Hampton, Country Carriers of West Surrey
18. Gertrude Jekyll, Old West Surrey (Facsimile Publishing, 1978)
19. Stephen Hampton, Country Carriers of West Surrey
20. P.A.L. Vine, Surrey Waterways (Middleton Press,1987)
21. P.A.L.Vine, London's Lost Route to the Sea, David and Charles, 1965
22. Cash Book of J. & J. Elliot
23. H.R. Hodd, The Horsham - Guildford Direct Railway (Oakwood Press 1975)
24. V. Mitchell & K. Smith, Branch Lines to Horsham (Middleton Press 1982)
25. Michael Miller, Around Cranleigh (Chalford,1996)
26. Post Office Heritage. Post Master General's Minute Book, Report no 237
27. John Elliot's school notebook,1838
28. Private Papers of Major D.S. Elliot
29. William Welch, *Cranley in 1846,* St. Nicolas Parish Magazine, 1896
30. Samuel Mann, Cranleigh in Ye Olden Days & Cranleigh Today
31. General Post Office Telephone Directory 1906. (B.T.Archives)

REFERENCES

Chapter 3: Cranleigh Families
 1. Thomas Moule, A topographical description of Surrey, 1837 (Historic Prints, 1912)

Chapter 4: Cranleigh's Children at School
 1. William Welch, *Cranley in 1846*
 2. Betty Seymour and Myrtle Warrington, Bygone Cranleigh (Philimore, 1984.)
 3. John Elliott's school notebook, 1938
 4. Circular letter appealing for money to build the National School, SHC, Ref. PSH/CRA/18/4
 5. Cranley National School Building Plans, 1847 and 1871, (SHC, Ref. 264/15/1-10.)
 6. Cranley National School Account Book, 1849-75, (SHC, Ref. 264/15/2.)
 7. Cranley National School Account Book, 1849-75, (SHS, Ref. 264/15/2.)
 8. Edwin Peters' Plan of Cranley National School, (SHC, Ref. 264/15/1-10)
 9. National School Admission Registers, 1848-56 and 1848-71, (SHC, Ref .6188/2/1.)
10. National School Admission Registers, 1856-71, (SHC, Ref. PSH/CRA/15/1.)
11. Betty Seymour and Myrtle Warrington, Bygone Cranleigh
12. National School Admission Registers, 1856-71,(SHC, Ref.PSH/CRA/15/1
13. Wilfred Colverson, Cranleigh - the Story of the Church and Parish of St Nicolas, (1977) Printed by Norman Starbuck of Cranleigh
14. National Society's Summary of the Capitation Class Register, 1868-71 and 1871-75, (St. N.)
15. Blogg papers, *The Beginnings of Education in Cranleigh in the Nineteenth Century,* (Rectory.)
16. National School Log Book, 1863-98, (St. N.)
17. National School Building Plans, 1847 and 1871, (SHC, Ref. 264/15/1-10.)
18. National School Register of Admission, Progress and Withdrawal, 1872-78, (St. N.)
19. National School Log Book, 1863-98, (St. N.)
20. National School Account Book, 1849-75, (SHC, Ref. PSH/CRA/15/2)
21. National School Log Book, 1863-98, (St N.)
22. National School Log Book, 1863-98, (St.N.)
23. National School Register of Admission, Progress and Withdrawal, 1893-1906, (St. N.)
24. National School Building Plans, 1847 and 1871, (SHC, Ref. 264/15/1-10.)
25. National School Surveyor's Report, 1905, (SHC, Ref. CC47/89)
26. National School Log Book, 1863-98, (St. N.)
27. National School Surveyor's Report, 1905, (SHC, Ref. CC47/89)
28. National School Punishment Book, 1909-80, (St. N.)
29. *School Days,* 1988, Glebelands School, Cranleigh
30. *Cranleigh - a Guide,* Cranleigh Chamber of Commerce, (c.1926.)
31. National School Punishment Book, 1909-80, (St. N.)
32. *School Days,* 1998, Glebelands School, Cranleigh
33. St. Nicolas Parish Magazine, 1926
34. National School Log Book, 1920-55, (St. N.)
35. We are grateful to Miss N. Budgett for this reminiscence.
36. National School Log Book, 1920-55, (St.N.)

REFERENCES

37. Blogg papers, *'Précis of Matters in Relation to Damage to Schools caused by Flying Bomb on 27-8-44'*, written by Mr. Blogg.
38. Blogg papers.
39. National School Punishment Book, 1909-80, (St. N.)
40. C.of E Primary School. Minutes of the Managing Body, 1937-68, (SHC,Ref. CEM/228/1.)
41. *'Our Schools in 1948'*, Blogg papers.
42. National School Log Book, 1955-85, (St. Nicolas School.)
43. National School Log Book, 1955-85, (St. N.)
44. *'Pageant Fayre'* programme, Blogg papers.

Chapter 5: Shopping
1. William Welch, *'Cranley in 1846'*, St. Nicolas Parish Magazine, 1896

ACKNOWLEDGEMENTS

The authors and editors would like to express their grateful thanks to the many people who have helped in the preparation of this book, particularly Janet Holt, Bob Mesley and Ron Phelps and to Don Simmons for generously allowing us to publish his work on the Cranleigh Village Hospital. Thanks to Glebelands School for the loan of 'School Days'; to Major David Elliot for permission to reproduce extracts from John Elliot's 1838 homework and notebook, the cash book of J.& J. Elliot and other personal papers; to the Reverend Nigel Nicholson for access to the Blogg papers and for permission to use material from the Cranleigh Parish Registers; to John Reading, Headmaster for documents kept at St. Nicholas school; to John Gallagher for the loan of original maps and to Nick Galpin for reproducing maps for publication; to Maurice Drake of Wellset, for his invaluable advice in preparing the book for publication; to the staff at the Surrey History Centre at Woking for their patience and help and finally, to Mr. Jowett, of The Bookshop for his generous help in selling the book.

Among the many who contributed personal reminiscences particular thanks to Phyllis Beeson, Miss N. Budgett, Brenda Clague, Roy Collins, Len Copus, Charles Croxford, Roy Foster, Esme Furman, Vic Philpot and Gordon Thomas.

For assistance with illustrations we are indebted to Michael Miller, to Robin Brand for the loan of photographs from David Mann's collection, to Mr. Harvey Ide, of the Cranleigh Camera Shop and to Miss C. Coombs, T. Disley, N. Hampshire, Pat Mills, Don Simmons, and Ian Stedman for access to material from private collections, and to Chris Baker and Arthur Wren. The advertisements for various Cranleigh shops have been reproduced from Lucas's Cranleigh Pictorial Guide and Directory, 1923. Extracts from GPO minute book reproduced by kind permission of Post Office Heritage. The authors and editors have made every effort to ensure that all materials used have been acknowledged and offer their apologies for any omissions.

BIBLIOGRAPHY

Primary Sources

Blogg papers. (Collection of Mr. Blogg's papers, held in St. Nicolas Rectory)

Cash Book of J. & J. Elliot. (Private papers of Major D. S. Elliot)

Census enumerators' books, Cranleigh 1851, (PRO, RG107/1597 1861,(PRO, RG9/228), 1871,(PRO, RG10/825), 1881,(PRO, RG11/799), 1891,(PRO,RG12/0572-3)

Cranley National School Account Book 1849-75 (SHC, 264/15/2)

Cranley National School Admission Registers, 1848-56 and1848-71, (SHC, Ref 6188/2/1) and 1856-71, (SHC, Ref PSH/CRA/15/1)

Cranley School Register, Admission and Progress and Withdrawal, (1848-1868) (SHC,CRA/15/1)

Cranley National School Building Plans 1847 and 1871, (SHC, Ref 264/15/1-10)

Cranleigh National School Log Books for 1863-98, 1898-1920, 1920-55 and 1955-85 (St. N.)

Cranleigh National School Punishment Book. 1909-80. (St N.)

Cranleigh National School Register of Admission, Progress and Withdrawal for 1872-78, 1874-92, 1886-1900, 1893-1906, 1900-12, 1921-32, 1932-41 and 1941- 49. (St. N.)

Cranleigh National School Surveyor's Report 1905 (SHC, Ref CCA47/89)

Cranleigh Poor Rate Book, (SHC, P58/4/2)

Cranleigh Register of Electors 1856/7 (SHC, QS/7/4), 1892 (SHC, QS74/1-10)

General Post Office Telephone Directory, 1906 (BT archives)

Illustrated London News, 5 April 1851

Kelly's Directories:1851, 1852, 1874, 1891, 1903, 1913, 1918, 1934

National Society's Summary of the Capitation Class Register, (Summary of Attendances, School fees etc.) for 1868-71 and 1871-75. (St. N.)

Post Office Heritage, Post Master General's Minute Book.

School notebook of John Elliot (Private papers of Major D S Elliot)

St. Nicolas Parish Magazines, 1896, 1906, 1926

Undertaking not to sell goods on Sunday. (SHC, Ref. PSH/CRA/18/4)

Secondary Sources

Belloc, Hilaire, The Stane Street, Constable, 1913

Best, Geoffrey, Mid-Victorian Britain 1851-75, Weidenfield and Nicolson, 1971. Fontana Press 1835, 3rd.imp

Budgen, Christopher, Bramley and Rudgwick Turnpike Trust (Surrey Archaeological Collection)

Budgen, Christopher, Cranleigh: A History of Wealden Settlement, Wealden Publishing, 1998

Cobbett, William, Rural Rides, 1830. Reprinted, Penguin, 1981

Colverson, William, Cranleigh: The Story of the Church and Parish of St Nicolas, 1977 (Printed by Norman Starbuck of Cranleigh)

Cranleigh and Ewhurst Pictorial Guide and Directory, Lucas, 1923

BIBLIOGRAPHY

Cranleigh: A Guide, Cranleigh and District Chamber of Commerce, 1932 and 1933

Cranleigh Cares, Cranleigh and District Chamber of Commerce, 1979 and 1981

Cranleigh Guide, Cranleigh and District Chamber of Commerce, 1958, 1967 and 1972

Cranleigh Monthly Medley Magazine (The), The Cranleigh Press 1912

Elliott's Cranleigh Directory and Almanac, F. P. Elliott, 1911

English, Judie, Cranleigh: A historical walk, 1985

Everitt, A., Country, county and town, Transactions of the RHS, 1979,

Gerhold, Dorian, Road Transport before the Railways, C.U.P., 1993

Hampton, Stephen Country Carriers of West Surrey: A Study of the Guildford Area 1850 - 1950, (Unpublished thesis submitted for M.A. degree in English Local History, Leicester University, 1971)

Hodd, H. R., The Horsham - Guildford Direct Railway, Oakwood Press 1975

Horn, Pamela, The Rise and fall of the Victorian Servant. Sutton Publishing, 1975

Jekyll, Gertrude, Old West Surrey, Facsimile Publishing, 1978

Lasham's Guildford Almanac 1851, 1859, 1882, 1903, 1912

Malden, H. E., (ed), The Victoria History of the Counties of England, Parts 12 & 14 (Constable 1912)

Mann, Samuel, Cranleigh in Ye Olden Days & Cranleigh Today, 1930. Southern Reprographics. Reprinted and updated 1985

Manning, Rev. Owen and William Bray, The History and Antiquities of the County of Surrey, (E. P. Publishing Ltd in collaboration with Surrey County Library. Reprinted 1974)

Megahey, A. J., A History of Cranleigh School, (Collins, 1983)

Miller, Michael, Around Cranleigh, Chalford Pub. Co., 1995

Mitchell, V. and Smith, K., Branch Lines to Horsham, Middleton Press 1982

Moule, T. A. Topographical Description of Surrey, 1837, Reproduced 1972, Stevens Historic Prints

Pryce, W.T.R.(ed) From Family History to Community History, Studying Family and Community History: 19th and 20th Centuries. Vol. 2. Series editor: Ruth Finnegan, C.U.P. in association with the Open University, 1994

Seymour, B and Myrtle Warrington, Bygone Cranleigh, Phillimore, 1984

Shamley Green History Society, A History of the Village, 1993

Swinnerton, Frank, Reflections from a Village, Hutchinson 1969

Vine, P. A. L., London's Lost Route to the Sea, David and Charles, 1965

Vine, P. A. L., Surrey Waterways, pub Constable, 1912. Reprinted Middleton Press, 1987

Viney, Gwen, Memories of Cranleigh, Entaprint, Cranleigh, 1985

Maps

O.S.1891, Surrey Sheet xxxix. 11

O.S. 1913, Surrey Sheet xxxix. 11

O.S. 1970, TQ0439/0539

Video

The Horsham and Guildford Direct Railway, Oakwood Video Library.

INDEX

INDEX

INDEX

INDEX

INDEX

SUBSCRIBERS

The following subscribers helpfully supported this publication with their contributions in advance of publication:

Alison and Julian Adams
Mrs. N. Addison
Mr. & Mrs. T. H. Ashton
Mari Bailey
Hilda Barker
Shirley Betteridge
Barbara Betts
E. Bickle
Daphne and Karl Bogelin
Peter Brierley
Keith and Liz Brook
Avis Brown
Joyce Butcher
Phyllis Byne
Mike Carter
Beryl Casey
Maeve Catford
P. S. Chadburn
Mr. &. Mrs. Ken Cheel
Audrey Clarke
Sheila Courshee
Cranleigh Library
Sheilah and Roger Daniell
Audrey Davenport
Peter Dawson
Terry Disley
Jean Dodd
Mrs. R. Dubois
Peter Dulley
Ray and Wendy Dunnett
Alison Few
M. Forristal
David Fricker
Jan and Alan Fricker
Sarah Fricker

Tom Fricker
Mrs. J. Fynn
Pauline Gallagher
Rosemary Gooding
Peter N. Goodwin
Joy Granger
Mrs. I. E. Grout
Guildford Library
Mrs. Harley
Gordon Hellyer
David and Rosemary
    Hickman
Janet Holt
Margaret and John Hurst
Sylvia Hyde
Mr. G. Jackman
J. C. Jackman
Vera Jenkins
Mrs. E. Jones
Elizabeth Kelsey
Sheila Keown
Olive Kernot
Mr. & Mrs. M. H.
    Lendrum
Jenny Lewis
Amy Loveless
Jean Miles
Paul, Lori and Max Miller
Michael and Pat Miller
David Mills
Margaret Morgan
Iris Morse
Jill Newcomb   ·
Terry Oyler
Betty and John Parry

Wendy Pennock
Ron and Betty Phelps
Barbara Pidgeon
Mrs. Pratt
Kitty Remnant
E. Rich, Shere Museum
Mr. & Mrs. G. Rollo
Jean Sandow
Celia and John Savage
Charles and Beryl Scott
Pat Seymour
Biddy Sheather
Mrs. Sheriff
Pat Smart
Mr. A. J. Smith
Irene Smith
Ms. S. A. Smith
Jackie Spong
Sylvia Stanbrook
Mr. & Mrs. K. J. Stevens
Brenda Stone
Mr. & Mrs. W. R. Thomas
Nola Thorne
Val and Tony Thorogood
Beatrice Tolley
Dr. R. D. Townsend
Andrew Tyson & family
Bob and Helen Tyson
Mrs. G. J. Vivers
Joyce Watson
Stella Estelle Wayne
Jean Welling
Mrs. J. Williams
Joan Winspear